xoxo

# Pu...

## Essays on Otherness

By
## Samantha Mann

Published by

Read
Furiously
Read Often. Read Well.

Published by Read Furiously. First Edition.

ISBN: 978–0–9965227–8–6

Essay Collection
LGBTQ+ Literature
Contemporary Women Writers

For more information on *Putting Out: Essays on Otherness* or Read Furiously, please visit readfuriously.com. For inquiries, please contact
samantha@readfuriously.com.

This book contains portions of *The Bell Jar* by Sylvia Plath, *The L Word* created by lene Chaiken, Michele Abbot and Kathy Greenberg, and lyrics from *Save Me* by Jem.

Cover and Layout by Liz Ablashi and Adam Wilson

Edited by Samantha Atzeni

Read (v): The act of interpreting and understanding the written word.

Furiously (adv): To engage in an activity with passion and excitement.

**Read Often. Read Well.
Read Furiously**

I have already lost touch with a couple of people I used to be.

**–Joan Didion,**
*Slouching Towards Bethlehem*

# Table of Contents

# Forward

I splattered pieces of some of these essays down nearly a decade ago. The thought or intention of publishing any of these splatterings wasn't an inkling of an intention. Allowing others to read my words was a nightmare scenario and the most mortifying experience I could imagine. This was a time when appearing to have it all together, at all times, no matter the cost was my main objective. Maintaining this was an exhausting and disconnected way to live as I couldn't possibly form strong bonds with others if I was never giving over an earnest part of myself.

Writing has always been the means in which to get *it* out. As I sat at my keyboard hour after hour, I didn't know what or why I was typing. It's never felt like writing has been a choice. I have memories of being young and feeling the compulsion to create. My second grade teacher agreed to let me stay inside during afternoon recess a few days a week to sit at the classroom computer using her story–creating program. The program let you choose visual backgrounds, characters, write dialogue and fill in story outlines. A memorable note from my friend during this year reads

*Sam, will you be at recess or are you working on a story?* It felt important and pertinent, story writing.

Countless moments and experiences transpired between the girl who couldn't even tell her best friends when she was having a bad day to the women who writes and publishes essays about the orgasm gap, self loathing, disordered eating, and casual sex. Many of the essays in this book are no longer reflections of me, which is wonderful as the stamina and loneliness it took to keep up with that young woman was soul–crushing. I still know her and acknowledge her as a part of me, but she is no longer in charge of driving the bus. Some days she still loudly flares up, but she's manageable.

With growth comes new dark corners and remnants of old wounds that still haven't fully healed, all on top of the new scars the world regularly doles out. A decade ago this truth would have felt devastating, but now I see this as a place to find new stories, connections with others, and hopefully enough time to lose myself all over again. Maybe my next book will be lighter and fueled more by witty observations than trauma and strife. I need to put out these essays, my innards, bones, guts, and broken parts to move forward.

Too often we attempt to combat the complexities of individual humans by putting one another in neatly labeled boxes. Our brains prefer organization, and although reductionist, labeling is the simplest way for us to make automatic judgments and sort one another into "us" and "them" groups. At first glance the most obvious label I wear is that of a woman, a white woman. While I identify as a Lesbian, this isn't immediately discernible as I appear typically gender–conformed for a person my age. I don't pretend to have the ability to YouTube video–Kardashian–level beat my face, but most mornings I manage to put on mascara and eyeshadow well enough. If I want to convince myself that I'm really trying, I can muster up the energy to add eyeliner. I'm of average weight, maybe on the smaller side depending on the city in which you live. For better or worse, I meet base expectations of the male gaze. I'm Jewish, but with mixed parents I undoubtedly pass as a shiksa. My labels of *Jew*, *women*, and *lesbian* categorize me as a marginalized person, but I recognize that my white privilege and gender conformity overrides many of these marginalized aspects on a day–to–day basis, and allows me to move through the world with relative ease compared to others. I have the luxury to be invisible when I want go unnoticed and feel unseen. Maneuvering through the physical world isn't especially difficult for me due to my outer layer of skin and the way in which I present myself.

This is not to say my personal life hasn't been painful and that every day my life blooms full of flowers and high fives, but I want to be clear about my privilege upfront. I also move through the world with a hardy combination of mental health issues, a history of sexual trauma, and an unfortunate need to please. This combination has plagued me with an overwhelming sense of being different from others. For most of my life, I never felt like I was enough of anything or that I fit nicely into any one particular social space. I felt like an outsider even amongst my friends. For years I held close secrets about myself for fear that revealing them would cause those around me to see my otherness too.

Samantha Mann

I've gone to great lengths to hide my sexuality and struggles with mental health. By hiding myself from others I hoped to also hide from myself. The secrets are suffocating. Humans are complicated and using labels and boxes serves as an uninteresting attempt to better understand each other and ultimately ourselves. I'd like to commit to the convoluted.

# Depression, Women, & Writing. A Brief Personal Overview

**A**s a child, I transitioned from the comfort of my stuffed animal dog and blanket to the assurance of books, with years of thumbsucking in–between. Even the idea of thumbsucking now warms the most primal parts of my brain. My thumb stayed lodged in my mouth resting on top of my front teeth for enough years that I required braces in 5th grade and developed a severely calloused knuckle, which lasted until sophomore year of college. According to child development experts, I sucked my thumb for too long, but psychologically speaking, I didn't suck it so long that I need to talk to my therapist about it today. For years, books and thumbsucking acted as my optimum coping mechanism. The combination provided me with the maximum amount of self–soothing and assurance. Around fourth grade I convinced myself to keep my thumb out of my mouth due to the social pressures of sleepovers. I wanted to be seen as a cool, edgy kid and I knew being curled up in my sleeping bag in the fetal position sucking on my thumb like a baby wasn't the way to create this illusion. I reasoned with myself, however, that if I ever became a POW or ended up shipwrecked on an island I could pick up my sucking habit again. As I ridded myself of immature soothing habits my need for books grew.

Growing up I always kept at least one book tucked under my pillow and others lined along my bed. Stories have always provided me a sense of belonging and physically surrounding myself with them added a layer of security. Even today as someone who loathes clutter and tchotchkes, I have a bit of habit for hoarding books. They take up the majority of the space in my bedside table, fill up unnecessary space on the shelves in my closet, and appear in every bag I carry. Looking at my bookshelf is meditative and organizes my brain faster than any mindfulness app.

It was inside the pages of books that I found where all the other freaks lived. I could see parts of myself – the ugly, scary parts – that I didn't see reflected back in my friends or in any of the bubbly sitcom families I watched on *TGIF*. Reading made me feel understood and less alone. Books provided me a concrete system in which I could more accurately rate my weirdness against the universe. Sure, I had a fight with my mom and thought she was insane, but I had nothing on Augusten Burroughs literally spending his childhood watching his mother dissolve into mania. Perhaps I had occasionally restricted my food intake, but Lauren Greenfield actually starved herself to the point that she grew a layer of fuzz all over her body. Once in middle school I showed my friends The Joy of Sex and one of them called me a pervert, but Chelsea Handler showed her friends how to masturbate. No matter how shameful I felt about myself, books provided me with the knowledge that somewhere in the world existed a human crazier, grosser, or just plain *more* than me. This truth served as an enormous gift. My obsession with the atypical human condition formed early due to reading. The notion that people could suffer and share it with others thrilled me. As someone who yearned to appear *totally fine* I marveled at the idea of authors examining themselves and then handing it over to the world completely out of their control. Early on I found a sense of revolution, comfort, and strength in words and writing.

I don't remember stumbling upon Sylvia Plath's *The Bell Jar*. No epiphany occurred where someone I admired gave it me with the promise of a literary awakening. No teacher assigned it to me. It simply always lived on my bookshelf and inside my brain. I have the same copy today that I had at age 13. Most likely I looted it from my mom's closest, as that's how I acquired many of my early books and cassette tapes. Some favorite cassettes included: TLC's *CrazySexyCool*, Garth Brooks' *Ropin' the Wind*, and The Original Motion Picture Soundtrack to the movie *Annie*. Countless nights I fell asleep with the *Annie* cassette in my hand and headphones still on listening to "I think I'm going to like it here" while I dreamed about twirling around an open ballroom space and sliding down the Warbuck's staircase with a cast of maids and butlers cheering me on. Often I sprang awake from fear that I would strangle myself with the thick headset cord while asleep. TLC's *CrazySexyCool* blasted from our family boombox as I made up dance routines with my next door neighbor. For the most part, the stolen tapes provided soothing experiences.

The books I lifted from my mother's closet included E.E. Cumming's *Tulips and Chimneys*, Frank McCourt's *Angela's Ashes*, which was the first book to make me cry, and one of my favorites books as a tween: Terry McMillan's *How Stella Got her Groove Back*. I re–read the first half of this book repeatedly as that's where all the sexy scenes took place. Stella made adulthood appealing and helped shaped my fantasy about having access to far off experiences like money, career, travel, and good sex. And while I only liked one poem in the entire collection of *Tulips and Chimneys*, I liked how E.E. Cummings looked on my bookshelf. I hoped the thick book of poetry gave off an intellectual vibe to my preteen friends. The pages smelled of must like an antique stores and even though it wasn't my favorite, I had a sense it had been well loved. My collection of contraband, while varied, brought about a sense of comfort to my world.

*The Bell Jar* was the first book that knocked the air out of me with its honesty, and helped me better understand parts of myself. It was a different than other books in that it wasn't comforting; it was illuminating, insightful and transformative. *The Bell Jar* and Plath gave me permission to be ambitious, arrogant, ungrateful, and ugly. Emotions that women are taught as too masculine Plath wore unabashed and didn't pretend like they didn't feel good. She gave me permission to be complex. Plath and her character Esther allowed themselves to sit in their sadness, which is a luxurious and novel idea for many of us; for women, sadness is something we are taught to always fight against.

I found myself drawn to her alternative lifestyle. Plath is essentially an amalgamation of the cast of *Girls* and *Sex In the City*, which is likely why so many females still obsess over her and she continues to feel relevant. Droves of women today don tattoos, necklaces, and tote bags paying homage to this woman and her ideas – just look at Etsy. Before *The Bell Jar*, I knew I experienced uncomfortable feelings, but I didn't have the vocabulary for it. Reading about depression for the first time as a despondent kid was an illuminating experience that allowed me to better comprehend myself in the world. All the morose thoughts and feelings I carried with me all at once openly displayed themselves in Plath's writing. For the first time, I realized my vague sense of sadness might not be unique. At 13, this realization brought me incredible relief.

I read *The Bell Jar* numerous times between the ages of 13 and 25. At this point, I cannot always decipher myself from Esther. I found, and continue to find, my occasional bouts of depression mystifying, the way Esther did. *I have all these things*, I would think to myself growing up; *a warm home, two parents, friends, lots of stuff, and an afterschool schedule full of extracurricular activities.*

I lived an enriched life, to say the least, and at times it felt as if my depression stemmed from not having enough gratitude and grace towards my comfortable upper middle class life. My parents exposed my brother and I to different types of people and places through travel and experiences. One summer they briefly contemplated taking us to Disneyland for a week, but nixed the idea when they realized we could rent a van and drive the entirety of Route 66 stopping at both

The Grand Canyon and Bryce National Park. The four of us crammed into the van seeing everything for the first time together is an unmatched experience. My mom appeared particularly giddy that trip. In my memories of her during those weeks she laughs, sings to the radio, and carries on in an uncharacteristically carefree manner; looking back I think she was falling in love with the Southwest. I spent time sitting in the front passenger seat journaling while my dad drove never trying to sneak a peek. I managed to make my six–year–old brother stop crying by drawing faces on my feet and performing a backseat puppet show. The van floor crunched beneath our small feet due to the accumulating layer of Goldfish cracker dust and granola bar crumbles.

I feel lucky to have many memories of being excited, happy, and safe growing up. I have other memories, however, when I felt the presence of something, which I would later discover to be "the bell jar," cover me seemingly out of nowhere, sucking out the color from my world. It would land on top of me one morning, distorting my view and dulling my sense of pleasure. A few days or weeks later, it would lift and I would assume every time that it was gone for good. As a teen, I didn't understand that this was depression operating. Isolation overwhelmed me during those foggy times. I hated seeing other people living their lives fully engaged in the moment and not trapped inside their heads. I could see these people and stand right beside them, but feel miles away.

My first heavy bought of depression settled in as my grandmother and I rode a train from Richmond,

Virginia to New York City the morning after Christmas. I was sixteen. We had excitedly planned this trip for months. My grandmother, who lived in California, and I talked on the phone putting together a meticulous itinerary for our three days and two night excursion. We overbooked our days and couldn't wait to see how much we could accomplish. The itinerary included obvious activities such as Katz Deli, the Rockettes Christmas Show, and shopping at Saks. We made an extended covert list also, which included wackier plans like buying pot in a head shop in the East Village and getting a piercing (neither of these plans materialized, although I do remember my grandmother having a frank discussion about buying some "grass" from a store clerk). My grandmother brought out a level of adventure in me that I loved to soak up.

*"Wherever I sat—on the deck of a ship or at a street café in Paris or Bangkok—I would be sitting under the same glass bell jar, stewing in my own sour air,"* Plath wrote.

These words rang inside of me as I sat on the train, filling up with anger. I hated myself for the sudden lack luster feelings. Here I was living my most exotic life, although not exactly Paris or Bangkok, and yet my feelings were still inescapable. I was horrified to figure out that no external experience, no matter how exciting or novel could repel feelings of emptiness.

Instead of my usual crazy excitement, I felt as if someone scooped all of my insides out; my brain had never felt so void of pleasure. My limbs felt packed with cement as I dragged them along the city streets. I lingered everywhere pretending to people watch or appear engrossed in the scene, but in reality, I just didn't have the energy to go on to the next activity. At every diner, museum, or park bench I tried to linger for as long as possible hoping it would cut down on our day. During each meal, I pretended to agonize over the menu in an attempt to stay put. My body just wanted to sit.

*Order everything you want to eat. We're on vacation*, my grandma said, trying be helpful. Embarrassment filled me going to bed each night knowing it was the easiest part of my day.

As I got older different parts of the book felt more salient: *"I guess I should have been excited the way most of the other girls were, but I couldn't get myself to react. I felt very still and very empty, the way the eye of a tornado must feel, moving dully along in the middle of the surrounding hullabaloo,"* Plath wrote. As a college student, it amazed me how much I could achieve while staying empty within.

Multiple semesters I attained an award for having the highest GPA in my sorority, I brought home new friends, and held multiple jobs throughout the summer and school year. Acting the part, no matter how my insides feel has always come naturally to me. Throughout entire relationships I've pretended to be content and happy at a passable level. If anything, I learned the achieving of external things left me feeling more hollowed out because now I had these accomplishments to look at. It seems less taxing and more appropriate to feel depressed about being a failure.

Like Sylvia Plath, I don't remember finding Virginia Woolf. The two women always lived side by side on my bookshelf and in my life. I obsessed over

*Mrs. Dalloway* and the minutiae of a single day. When *The Hours* came out, it felt as if Michael Cunningham had written a secret handbook for sad women. My one other depressed friend and I would read sections aloud to one another on the phone attempting to find the quotes that matched our sunken–in selves best. No one understands the agony of a single hour more than a depresso, and realizing other people existed that understood that meant everything.

While unarguably brilliant, Sylvia Plath, Virginia Woolf, and various other female authors also suffered with mental illness that eventually took their lives. As a young woman, I swung between glorifying and agonizing over their suicides. At times I assumed that without their insufferable mental experiences they wouldn't have been able to access what was required to create their works. It was easy to romanticize the deaths of these women writers since often times, like their work, their deaths spoke loudly and held my attention. It felt like these women's suicides acted as their final endeavor in storytelling. Other times, I agonized over their deaths and feared that suicide was the only solution to a life of feeling too different and sinking too deep into depression. It shocked me to think about how these women who were so brilliant yet still could not find an alternative solution to their pain. I projected my own fears of not being able to withstand myself onto their untimely endings.

The poet Anne Sexton donned a fur coat and carefully selected pieces of her mother jewelry to wear before she took her life. Glamour and pompous exist in this act whether we agree with it or not. Sylvia Plath stuck her head inside an oven while her two children played in the next room. This action can easily be seen as one final rage against the patriarchal society she pushed back against her whole life. Thinking about Virginia Woolf calmly walking into a lake as she filled her pockets with stones remains one of the most haunting and strangely beautiful visuals in my mind. These women refused to go out unseen. Today the debate continues among artists with mental illness themselves: *do I need this to create?*

More and more the answer seems to be no. People do not have to suffer and ultimately die for their best work to emerge, which is not to say it isn't helpful to have distant parents or a creepy uncle to get the initial creative juices going. Being a human is a traumatic event, so everyone is qualified to create. Trauma is simply a life event that changes your being on a cellular level and transforms the way in which you view the world. This can be not getting asked to prom, finding out Santa isn't real, being raped, losing a loved one, and any of life's other in–between moments.

I've often wondered what would have come after *The Bell Jar*. Plath took her life at age 30, so we missed out on decades of experiences from her. Today she would be 83, meaning that in an alternative universe, Plath could have had a Twitter account and marched with Gloria Steinem at the Women's March in Washington, DC. What would she have added to the conversation about the work/motherhood balance and the importance of intersectionality in fourth wave feminism? While maybe a statement, her death isn't romantic nor should we feel like her death elevates her work. Women need to keep writing and to do so, we must be present. We must be alive. Our experiences need to be seen and heard as we have centuries of male driven storytelling to make up for. We can't write, however, if we've crammed our head into an oven or sat ourselves in a running car in a closed off garage.

Feeling like you no longer have options or will never feel joy again is one of the most difficult parts of depression. It feels all–consuming and real, but it's a lie. No feeling, good or bad, remains permanent and we always have options. I realize I wrote this today, on a good day, as a reminder. I know that on bad days, optimism may not be as easy to access. Most importantly, we should know not to trust ourselves to the fullest extent when we're in "the bell jar." It's only you in there after all. You don't have anyone to bounce ideas off of, and you're probably going a little stir crazy. Find a stone and throw it. Smash it. Ask for help. Get out. Create something. Just don't put those stones in your pocket and go looking for the nearest river.

# Seriously, I'm Kidding

**B**efore pop culture, boys, and the "shoulds" of our mothers overpower us, girls have a window of time to engage in their most natural curiosities. For many of my friends and me our early hobbies included nature exploration, light witchcraft, and repetitively creating our own sacred spaces in the forms of outdoor forts, basement clubhouses, and our bedrooms. Although they can't be accurate, I have memories of playing the game *light as a feather, stiff as a board* and it actually working on multiple occasions. I can vividly see my petite friends floating above the ground while a group of us circled around her chanting. The fact that many girls start out believing they are powerful witches only proves to the destructive influence of the damaging culture we raise them in. As girls, we transition from trusting our own supernatural aspects and valuing the strength of friendship to viciously turning on each other and ourselves in less than a handful of years. The external forces that fracture us speaks to society realizing and being fearful of the awesome power that a cohesive group of women hold. It has long served in the best interest of men to keep women separate and feeling powerless.

We should have kept practicing witchcraft in covens instead of joining the cheerleading squad.

Today the window of time that girls have to run, jump, read, and nerd out in whichever subject area they choose is becoming smaller. You're lucky if you can lose yourself to societal pressures for a period of time, eventually finding your way back to that weird girl you used to be, all by the time you reach your mid–to–late twenties. At twelve, my best friend and I sat in open construction sites writing hilarious erotic poetry pretending we inhabited the empty two stories homes. Just three years later, we will spend most of our time trying to impress boys and make each other jealous.

In sixth grade my friends and I lived between these two worlds. We were slowly losing our grip on our carefree disheveled–haired selves in favor of the Britney Spears sexy idea of an adult woman. Sixth grade was the last year we inhabited both of these conflicting internal spaces. For my twelfth birthday party, I begged for a sleepover. I always wanted a sleepover birthday party. Nothing felt better to me than having my best friends over to stay up as late as we could to pull silly pranks and obsessively discussing our favorite topics: "sex," our current bodies, our future bodies, and boys. Pranks usually involved a tampon, condom, or whatever adult paraphernalia we could access. One time we each decorated a tampon and then sent the whole fleet of them afloat in my neighborhood lake betting on which "boat" would expand and sink first – our own regatta.

Another time we soaked a box of tampons in water dyed with red food coloring. We then took turns using the blow dryer to dry them out, which took quite a bit of time due to quality absorption. Once they dried we snuck out and hung them in a tree of the yard of this girl we hated. We blew up condoms to use in a makeshift game of volleyball and stretched them out over our feet in an attempt to use the lubricated tubes as sliding socks (this doesn't work*). The cruelest prank we ever pulled was calling a taxi to one of our teacher's homes in the middle of the night. Over the phone in a hack British accent, my friend Sara* explained to the taxi company she would likely be sleeping so they might need to ring the doorbell multiple times if the honking didn't make her come out. A different night we ordered ten pizzas to this same teacher's home. I can't remember if we hated this woman or wanted to befriend her as those emotions felt similar in sixth grade.

Some nights a group of us would share two strawberry–daiquiri flavored Seagram's Wine. Then the entire bunch of us would proceed to run topless up and down our quiet neighborhood streets at 3 a.m., convinced we were drunk. At twelve our breasts collectively ran from size *just nipple* to full C. Everyone loved being topless under the protection of the night sky. It's not often girls get to feel fresh air on their bare chests the way boys frequently do. The act rang of rebellion and freedom. We were at an age when we weren't overly self–conscious around each other because our own sense of body hatred hadn't quite settled in. This allowed us to intrusively inspect one

14

another without caution. Lara*, who rang in at breast size *just nipple*, routinely would grab an entire fistful of breast belonging to another girl seething with jealousy. *I pray every night for these*, she said with her hand full of my friend Emma's* left breast. Knowing her family as overtly religious I genuinely believe this prayer was a part of her nightly ritual. I was personally fascinated in seeing the variety of nipples – like snowflakes, no two were identical. After, doodling penises on whichever girl fell asleep first was an obvious requirement.

Sleepovers felt like a practice for what I hoped adulthood would be like; freedom. It was the one time when my parents left me mostly unattended, and we had hours of uninterrupted time to chatter loudly and endlessly. At a recent sleepover at Emma's* house, she told us, in a ghost story–like fashion, about how her cousin had let a boy finger her. *And then he put his finger inside of her…vagina. And then… she totally liked it!* She said screeching. We all screamed with disgust and swore we would never allow a boy to put his finger inside of us, and if it did happen we vowed to never enjoy it. *Unless he's going to do something helpful, like put a tampon up there, then I just don't see the point*, Katie*, a girl one year older than most us, said with authority. We all nodded in agreement at her sage knowledge. Soon we'll all see the movie *Fear* and watching Reese Witherspoon's face transform on that fateful roller coaster ride with Marky Mark will have us all questioning our initial suspicions about fingering.

My buddy Amanda*, who later will devote her life to international missionary work, taught us all how to smoke cigarettes without coughing at another memorable sleepover. Spoiler: you just hold the smoke in your mouth and then blow it out in a lackadaisical fashion. She also taught us how to hold a proper séance, which essentially is just lots of salt, handholding, and screaming at one another to not break hands in the circle. During one particularly spooky séance, Amanda*, Sara*, and I sat in Amanda's* garage and tried to summon up Sara's* father who had recently passed away. A gust of wind from seemingly nowhere slammed the kitchen door shut blowing out the candle. Sara* cried hysterically for the rest of the night, and we never held another séance, as it turned out we possessed too much power. Sleepovers were a transient place we created to learn and explore all the possibilities that lay ahead of us.

My twelfth birthday party was extra exciting because my parents had recently cleared out our attic and turned it into a play space for my brother and me. The perimeter of the attic was stacked with typical suburban attic boxes: Christmas decorations, Halloween decorations, 100–year–old antique family crib that my mom had already convinced me I would want for a child of my own someday, dressers that were out of style but maybe we would need later, boxes of my parent's childhood memorabilia, and dusty luggage. My parents put a Berber carpet down in the middle of the room taking up about 12 feet one way and 15 feet the other way. They added my brother's wooden Brio train table and two plastic chairs designed for miniature preschool bodies. It was May in Virginia, which meant it was almost too hot to stay alive up there, but the feeling of secrecy overrode the heat so we kept ourselves locked up in the attic for hours. We drank pink lemonade crystal light by the gallon and devoured ice pops to keep cool. Just as we were laughing about how disgusting pubic hair must be my mom shouted up that dinner would be ready in five minutes. As we were cleaned up the room and got ready to head downstairs the silliest idea occurred to me.

*I have a big announcement to make,* I said proudly.

*What is it?* everyone asked excitedly.

*You guys will have to wait until dinner, I want my parents to hear it too,* I said with a smirk.

As we walked down the stairs into the kitchen my dad shouted, *There's the birthday girl!* He was holding our family camcorder and waving at my friends and me.

My face flushed with excitement when I saw the camera. I needed to time my announcement perfectly I thought. This is going to be the funniest thing I've ever said, and it's going to be recorded. *I have to tell everyone something important,* I said facing the camera and smiling from ear to ear.

*Great, what is it bug?* My mom said beaming as she finished setting the table.

*Well, I wanted to tell you guys that I'm gay. Like how Uncle Adam is gay.* I said completely stone–faced. Then, for fifteen long seconds everyone was silent. *Maybe I shouldn't have said that,* I thought. *Does everyone think I'm gross?* I wondered as I started to panic. I held my breath and then in what felt like a lifetime later all my friends began to howl. I let out a sigh and giggled too.

My giggle turned into a belly laugh, and soon I was laughing so hard I began crying tears composed of equal parts genuine laugher and enormous relief.

My friends keeled over completely beside themselves. I saw Emma* literally slap her knee; it was clearly the funniest thing they had ever heard. My bit had killed.

Knowing that the camera was still rolling my friend Katy* jumped in front of it and pretended to hold a microphone news reporter style and grabbed me. *Now Sam, you have just announced that you're gay. What else can you tell us about this? How gay are you?* She said in her best news anchor voice, attempting to maintain her professionalism. At this point, the rest of my friends were rolling on the floor screaming with laughter. Everyone was gasping for breaths.

My parents, who had not said a word, were making eyes at each other from across the kitchen. The camera continued to film. *Well the technical term is lesbian,* I said back to Katy* in my best serious interview voice. *But to answer your question, I am very gay. Maybe the gayest. Ellen got nothing on me* I said and threw up a peace sign at the camera.

The interview abruptly ended when my dad turned off the camcorder. I wiped the joyous snot and tears away from my face and helped my friends off the floor. We managed to settle in at the kitchen table, but periodically would break into hysterics throughout the meal. My friend Katie* spit out a chunk of burger during one laughing break, which ramped us all back up. It's a miracle no one choked to death during dinner that night. My parents never mentioned my announcement again. They didn't even ask me to clarify it the next morning after everyone went home. I stayed on edge for days thinking one of them would bring it up, but nothing happened.

Today, I have no idea why I said it. I've sat with this moment for countless hours, but still haven't been able to come up with a meaningful explanation for myself. Did I simply think it would be an amazing bit; I was an attention seeker. On some level did I know I was gay? Did I want to see how it felt to say out loud? Either way, I wouldn't make that announcement again for a solid decade.

I like to think that hearing my friends laugh with me while "coming out" helped give me the courage to repeat those same words to many of those exact women and my family again 10 years later. I like to believe this moment acted as a safe dry run that I held onto somewhere deep in my brain. Before calling my parents to actually out myself at age 22, I sat on the floor of my apartment closet nervously inhaling a six–pack of Natty Light revisiting this childhood moment. *You've literally already done this* I thought to myself laughing out loud like a young woman on the edge of freedom or a mental breakdown. I reexamined my initial "coming out" experience searching for reassurance.

Even though everyone laughed when I made my announcement, no one responded with disgust or disapproval. While my parents didn't respond at all, they also didn't send me the message that being gay wasn't an option. No sit–down took place where they talked to me about "morality" or pushed any agenda on what they thought an acceptable life for me would look like. They didn't even reprimand me for the joke, which sent the message that maybe this gay stuff wasn't that big of a deal. Saying *I'm gay* out loud as a small 12–year–old girl felt powerful and electrifying. I'm not sure if it was due to releasing something deeply true inside of myself, or if it simply felt amazing to hold the attention of a room and make everyone laugh until they cried. Coming out 10 years later to many of those same people felt similar. It was a huge relief and laughter filled much of the conversation.

# Bewitched

Throughout my early existence I craved complex relationships with the adults in my life. By complex, I mean I wanted adults to see me as an equal, desire me sexually, or – at the very least – I wanted to make them laugh. Even today, nothing feels more satisfying than making someone giggle. I found this especially powerful as a child. Making an adult laugh as a child felt like tapping into their secret world, if just for a moment. Laughing builds a connection with someone and shows you understand specificity about him or her. Intimacy and laughter have long been synonymous for me. Early on I balked at formal boundaries and felt the compulsive need to smash the lines between "us" and "them."

This need to insert myself into the adult world manifested itself primarily as a preoccupation with teachers and coaches. While generally, any reference to borderline pedophilia in movies and music makes me want to smash in car windows and light entire city blocks on fire, the Police song "Don't Stand So Close to Me" and Gary Puckett and The Union Gap's "Young Girl" resonated like dream scenarios for me.

I wanted to be the younger women making adults have confusing feelings forcing them to question their morality. Please tell me I'm irresistible and make you feel like leaving your wife and children while risking ruining your reputation and career! Older peers, while technically out of bounds, didn't appeal as much; maybe that idea was too attainable seeing as I've always automatically set over reaching expectations for myself.

In elementary school I first noticed I possessed a knack for talking to parents. The ease in which I could chat about grueling extracurricular schedules and unruly siblings impressed the neighborhood moms. *These state tests seem to get more involved every year,* I said to Mrs. Kelly at her breakfast table one morning.

*Too much emphasis on facts and not enough on critical thinking,* she added eagerly.

*I'll talk to her,* I said in an attempt to console Mrs. Griffin while sipping a soda on her couch while her daughter, Sandy, showered upstairs. *Between you and me, she's been having a difficult time since Billy dumped her for Rebecca in front of everyone during kickball last week,* I added.

*I really appreciate it,* Mrs. Griffin said to me misty—eyed. *Sandy's lucky to have a caring friend like you.*

*And don't worry,* she added, *I won't even mention that we spoke, you know how she gets.*

*Trying the new Weight Watchers system? My mom's been very successful with the new points systems. I'll have her send over her turkey cutlet recipe. Your kids will love it.* I said to a thankful Mrs. Peters in the front seat of her van as she drove a gaggle of us to the mall. It felt like a magic trick, getting adults to take me seriously. I found the situations compelling, and this initial interaction with parents acted as a stepping–stone in my need to push the line with adults.

It's easy to psychoanalyze my infatuations with adults as a symptom of early childhood sexual trauma, however, I've always believed the film *Matilda* deserves some culpability for these crushes. The year *Matilda* screened, I was eight and couldn't watch it enough. The film pushed me deeper into a lifelong love of books and libraries. Realizing you could lose yourself in a story and gain knowledge that no one could take away from you transformed how I moved through my world. No matter what happened around me I had books to hide in and new things to learn. After around 100 viewings, I began to believe that maybe I possessed Matilda–like magical qualities, and I started attempting to tap into my brain's ability for telekinesis. *Tip over glass, tip over glass, tip over,* I would repeat again and again, just like in the movie, as I concentrated on pushing over a glass of water with my mind while squinting my eyes for the full effect. I even readily convinced my younger brother that I had magical Matilda–like abilities. The best trick I created was an elaborate ploy to make items in our home "disappear" and "reappear." Typically, this involved me hiding and later revealing large toys like train sets, a PlayStation, and a dollhouse. He was spooked and impressed. He was also four.

Magic tricks and books aside; my favorite part of the movie was Matilda's teacher, Miss Honey. Miss Honey was the most beautiful woman I had ever seen and she lit my first flames of arousal. Despite her floral sack of a dress and bottle cap glasses, Miss

Honey had skin that looked soft and warm eyes that seemed like they could see into anyone's best parts. While not objectively gorgeous, something about her physical being caught my attention. She embodied a gentle spirit and helped Matilda realize she was an intelligent worthy human, not the freak her parents made her believe she was. Miss Honey made Matilda feel important and loved, and I found her dazzling. During the film Matilda teaches Miss Honey how to access her inner badass, and gives her the strength to stand up for herself. Seeing a small girl helping an adult woman to lead a braver life looked empowering, and I yearned for their dynamic.

At the end of the movie Miss Honey adopts Matilda, saving her from her wretched family. A scene depicts the two of them rearranging furniture and dancing to upbeat pop music with bandanas tied around their heads. My brain processed the scene as one of romance not friendship. I longed to be adopted by Miss Honey, however, at the end of my movie I wanted this adoption to blossom into true love and marriage. My brain fantasized about lying in bed with Miss Honey squeezing me tight and kissing me passionately on the mouth. Eventually, this fantasy fixation rolled over into infatuations with my actual schoolteachers. Throughout my educational career, I pined for beautiful female teachers aching for their attention. It began with benign crushes on my elementary school teachers. I merely wanted to be liked more than the other students. On occasion I would feel a sting of jealousy if I knew a teacher was keen on a specific student, but overall my feelings stopped at wanting to be adored the most.

My first sexual crush on a teacher occurred in my 8th grade Social Studies class. This crush would hit me harder and hurt more than any other, as first crushes do. In middle school we revolved on a block schedule, meaning we took half of our classes one day and the other half the next day, except for homeroom, which we attended every morning. By chance, I had Mrs. Alexander's Social Studies class for homeroom. Mrs. Alexander was the new teacher at our school and she presented herself as petite and uncomfortably shy. She physically reminded me of Miss Honey in both her sweet face and anxious mannerisms. She fumbled through lectures and repetitively cleared her throat while engaging in eye contact that could be classified as fleeting at best. Mrs. Alexander spoke with hesitation and stood at the front of the room with little authority. She was quick to blush. However, her lack of authority translated into students not giving her a hard time because the coursework didn't require much brainpower, and she let us pick our seats which was a very cool teacher move in eighth grade. It didn't hurt that assignments had flexible due dates and most quizzes were open book.

Similar to any obsessive love story, I don't recall exactly when I fell for her. I only know that once I did, it was all consuming and made me feel constantly flustered. Every time I spoke to her I could feel the heat rising up through my chest and spreading across my face up to the top of my ears. Maintaining eye contact was difficult if not impossible. Each morning I would feed my friends an elaborate excuse of why I needed to get to class before the first bell rang. I couldn't let them know I was a teacher–obsessed freak. As I power walked down the hallway, I buzzed with excitement. I couldn't wait to say *good morning* and see how she wore her hair that day. Sitting in the empty classroom I prayed Mrs. Alexander would say anything to me. Some days I felt brave enough to attempt small talk, and I would ask her about an assignment, or I would act confused about a recent topic. My grandmother repeatedly told me throughout my adolescence to act like I didn't know how to do something if I wanted boys to like me. *I ask your grandfather how to do at least three things a day that I already know how to do. Men love it,* she said to me over countless phone calls. I routinely played dumb, hoping this universal Jewish grandmother truth would work on Mrs. Alexander too.

The whole time I crushed on Mrs. Alexander, I knew she was married. Aside from the obvious "Mrs." she would occasionally mention *him* on a Monday morning if the two of them did an activity over the weekend she felt was appropriate to share with the class. Every time she brought *him* up my insides felt as if they had been set on fire and my heart muscle tightened. I loathed this mystery husband. During math class, I often daydreamed about Mrs. Alexander realizing I was truly the love of her life and kicking Mr. Alexander out of the house so I could move in.

In my fantasy I imagined myself arriving to her front porch with one overpacked suitcase and her greeting me with a huge smile and wrapping me up in her arms. Kissing me, she would tell me that she had never felt happier. We would ride to school together every morning, oblivious to the stares as we would be too wrapped up in our bubble of love. The school would gossip about our relationship, but we wouldn't care. Just like in *Matilda*, I imagined us rearranging her living room furniture to make space for silly montage–style dance parties. Of course, these dance parties would end with us making out on her couch, and then ordering pizza for dinner because we would be too busy kissing to bother cooking. This elaborate delusion developed a few years after the Mary Kay Letourneau scandal, so it seemed like anything was possible. I had read every detail I could find about the Mary Kay Letourneau story, and it seemed to me that Billy and Mary Kay were truly soul mates. I believed our love could be ageless too. While Mrs. Alexander seemed to take a liking to me, I knew I needed to get more one–on–one time with her to win her away from her husband.

On Thursday afternoons, I had dance classes right after school, which required me to bring in a large duffle bag full of tights, leotards, and multiple shoes to school. I previously stored this duffle bag in my locker, but one morning realized that this oversized bag could be the key to getting me extra face time with Mrs. Alexander. One Thursday morning, I excitedly went to her class before the first bell and asked if I could leave my bag in her room for the day since it was interfering *so* much with my locker space. In reality, my locker remained mostly empty aside from two boxes of tampons, extra underwear, and a bagged lunch. I hadn't yet gotten my period, but I felt positive it lurked right around the corner. Having boxes of tampons was also important because I wanted to be a hero and have a spare for any girl in crisis. I imagined this scenario bringing the most popular girl in school and I together leading us to become besties. Unfortunately, the tampon boxes remained sealed all year.

Mrs. Alexander graciously allowed me to store my dance duffle in her classroom, instantly making Thursday my favorite day of the week. In the afternoon when I went to pick up my bag I would linger around and ask her how her day was. She began to offer me small pieces of chocolate from her desk, and I started believing that a true friendship was growing, which would quickly lead to her loving me and us kissing on her couch. As the weeks progressed, our Thursday afternoons became chattier. I disclosed silly stories about the drama among my friends and kept her in the loop of all the couples in our grade. I loved making her laugh. Her cheeks would often blush which made me feel like I had the power to make her uncomfortable. Looking back, I think she was just a socially awkward adult who had probably spent a lifetime blushing when laughing. Gaining personal information from her was difficult, but I did learn that she had a dog and that her husband was a dentist.

Our Thursday afternoons continued in the fashion of sharing chocolates and laughing about middle school and its many turmoils. I started to daydream of her husband committing suicide (I had heard that dentists had the highest suicide rates of all professionals), and I would be there to sweep up her broken heart and bring her back to life with a new love. Then one morning in the late third quarter of the year I felt a shift with

Mrs. Alexander. I dropped off my bag as usual, but she looked distracted and hardly smiled when I said *hello*. I told her I would see her that afternoon and I hoped she had a good day – to no response. Maybe he had left her. Maybe my moment had arrived! I planned for our future all day and practically sprinted to her room after the last bell of the afternoon rang.

As I entered the room, embarrassingly out of breath, she didn't look up. Her posture was that of a professor deep in the zone of grading papers, but her eyes looked out in the distance, not down at her stack, distracted. To me, it was the look of someone lost in the wreckage of her newly imploded life. Accidentally, on purpose, I hip checked the desk next to me causing her to break her stare from oblivion. I laughed and smiled trying to appear silly and clumsy…this seems like another piece of flirting advice my grandmother likely gave me. Pushing my hair behind my ears as a nervous habit, I asked her if she was okay and told her she looked sad. This was it; I was ready to console her and hold her while she wept and told me about her failed marriage and broken heart. She looked at me more serious than she ever had before. I felt my heart beating in my palms.

*I'm pregnant,* she said. *About three months.*

Her face quickly transformed into an excited beam as she asked me not to tell any other students as she wanted to make the announcement herself the next morning. Mrs. Anderson chatted casually holding a stupidly happy smile and mentioning she would take some time off at the beginning of next school year. My chest knotted and my stomach sank. My eyes burned as I willed back tears. Breathing in her hair, I gave Mrs. Anderson a hug and congratulated her.

No suicide or divorce, and I knew I wouldn't be her hero. I went back to storing my dance duffle inside my empty locker. No longer did I run to her class each morning before the bell, instead I idled in the hallway with my friends feeling typical and deflated. Each month as her stomach grew I felt further away from her. I attempted to begin untangling myself from the fantasy I had created. My mom bought a variety of onesies splashed with ducks, bears, and other neutral baby elements for me to bring in as a gift, and looked perplexed when I acted like I didn't want to bring them to her. *She's meant so much to you this year,* my mom insisted. On one of the last lagging days of the school year, I arrived to Mrs. Alexander's class before the first bell, an act I hadn't done in months. She shout me a big grin from her across the room when she saw me. My brain began to register this as a face one makes when seeing a good friend, not a lover. *This is the first gift we've received! Thank you so much,* she said giving me a squeeze.

The *we* stung despite the overwhelming evidence pointing the inevitability of an *us. Keep in touch, and good luck in high school.* Over the summer I was easily able to find her home number in the phone book, which led me to calling and hanging up after the first ring. Eventually, I graduated to calling, waiting for a voice, and then hanging up. After hearing Mr. Alexander's voice on the machine telling me no one was home for the 20th time, I felt exasperated and ready to let go. One afternoon late in August I watched a TV special on Mary Kay and Billy and for the first time I understood that Mary

Kay had played the prominent role in initiating their scandal of a relationship. In that moment I realized that the idea of seducing Mrs. Alexander was solely my imagination and the one-sidedness of it all made me feel idiotic.

Years later, I will finally fall in love with an age appropriate woman who happens to be a teacher. We will get married and I will watch her move through her career as a teacher, vice principal, and eventually a principal of a successful school. I like to think my 14-year-old self would be impressed with this fact. Even my best 8th grade fantasies didn't think to aim so high.

# Challah If You Hear Me

Seventh grade is a magical time for Jewish tweens who attend Sunday school regularly and are scheduled to be Bat/Bar Mitzvah. Almost every weekend of every month is crammed full of parties. Essentially, this ritual ends up acting as a dry run for all the weddings you will attend in the future. Your parents buy you beautiful dresses and your mom lets you borrow her pearl earrings. It feels very adult to attend mass amounts of events that include hors d'oeuvres, sit down dinners, dancing, and readings from the Torah.

*Your haftorah portion sounded beautiful,* I would say to my classmate during their afterparty. I had heard my best friend's mom, Mrs. Steinman, say this once and loved how it sounded. In reality, none of us listened as our peers stood on the bimah reading from the Torah and leading the service. We usually ducked down in one of the back pews playing M.A.S.H on the back of the program trying not to laugh too loud.

In the span of one year I attended at least twenty–five Bar/Bat Mitzvahs in which I ate approximately 150 Swedish meatballs, 75 miniature crab cakes, and ingested countless Shirley Temples. My best friend Emma and I would drink Shirley Temples at the same quick pace we would later drink vodka–club sodas in college. Usually about an hour into a party, Emma and I would sneak out to explore whatever space we inhabited for the evening, usually a local hotel or country club. On most occasions our explorations resulted in nothing more than stealing unnecessary items from the cleaning ladies' carts. Upper middle class girls love the thrill of stealing things they don't need; see films *Girl, Interrupted*, *Thirteen*, and *Bling Ring*. Perhaps the false sense of safety and order fostered by our polished suburban environment creates the need to behave in a way unaligned with community norms. The thrill of pocketing a lip balm you could pay for with your babysitting money serves as metaphysical *F–U* to the pressure of the burbs. Perfectionist pressure bubbles everywhere in these Type A environments, just think about Winona Ryder. The woman lived in the most suffocating pristine bubble of all – Los Angeles – and sometimes a girl needs to pocket $5,000 worth of swag from SAKS to feel like she can breathe.

Often times, after our raids we would redecorate a hallway or elevator with lifted toilet paper and tampons. One night while lurking around we struck gold by stumbling upon the hotel's "night club." By nightclub, I mean hotel bar that once a week hired a D.J. and plugged in a set of strobe lights. We managed to sneak in and dance with older men traveling on business for about two minutes before a bouncer escorted us out. No hard feelings on our end; getting kicked out was just as thrilling as sneaking in. One Saturday night towards the end of March, the middle of Bar Mitzvah season, as Emma and I sucked down our fourth Shirley Temple of the evening and took a break from dancing the Cupid Shuffle she asked me if I ever thought about Jesus.

*Jesus? Like Jesus Christ the Lord and Savior?* I asked.

*Yeah, like why don't we have Jesus? Do you think we're missing out on something?* She asked carelessly.

I started to laugh but then felt stunned. I had never considered any other religion. What if I was missing out on something? How could I publicly commit to Judaism without knowing what else was available to me? For the next few weeks this became all I thought about and stressed over. I needed to know more. Did I even want to be Jewish? I started googling Christian religions and tried to figure out what, if anything, Judaism lacked. After an exhaustive 5 minute Google search, I realized maybe I wanted to be Catholic. I loved the idea of heaven and this was an idea the Jews didn't offer up. From what I had learned, Jews allegedly went wherever God was after they died. This vague idea had perplexed me for years. It just wasn't concrete enough. This lack of a puffy–cloud–family–and–friends–filled heaven had allowed adult level existential angst to set in me by the time I turned ten. Believing in Heaven seemed like a way to rid myself of that. My research concluded that in order to get into Heaven all you had to do was follow some basic rules, and complete as many tenets as possible. This all seemed reasonable to me.

In middle school Emma and I accounted for at least half of our school's entire Jewish population.

We had attended different elementary schools, so before her I was used to being Jewish student 1 of 1. In elementary school I would lie to my teachers and classmates insisting to every one I could write perfectly in Hebrew. I would write my peer's names on the chalkboard impressing everyone with my knowledge of a second language. In reality I just phonetically wrote out the Hebrew letters that matched their English names. While I knew I was sort of lying, I didn't care and loved the attention. Besides, even as a kid I knew no one could fact check me. In December, I would bring in my menorah, give out chocolate gelt, and teach everyone how to play Dreidel. In elementary school we still maintained genuine excitement for each other's differences. Once in middle school, however, everyone began clinging to sameness as a sense of security. At the very least you needed to assimilate with your particular friend group whether they categorized themselves as jocks, nerds, sluts, or Goth kids. And most of our friends were Christians.

During this time at my middle school, Christianity acted not only a religion, but also a cool social activity. The Christian kids had their own after school clubs and coed summer camps where they slept in boxcars with actual electricity. At my Girl Scout summer camp, we slept in miniature tents half a foot off the ground and lacked both boys and AC. I had two good friends at the time who were heavily involved with Jesus and Christian activities. They squealed with excitement when I told them my news about wanting to be Catholic. After school one day they came over to help me decorate my room in a more Christian manner. Essentially this involved typing Bible quotes out in Comic Sans, printing them out, cutting them in fun designs, and then taping the quotes all over my room. The one above my light switch read, "John 8:12 Then spoke Jesus again to them, saying, I am the light of the world: he that follows me shall not walk in darkness, but shall have the light of life," obviously. I felt great about my newfound Catholicism. The assurance of knowing that there was a Heaven, my new awesome bedroom decor, and the promise of a coed summer camp convinced me that I could readily give up Judaism. I would have to tell my parents to cancel the Bat Mitzvah. In the car ride home after a Hebrew lesson, I broke the news.

*Mom. I think I'm Catholic. I don't think I will be able to go through with my Bat Mitzvah,* I said coolly, though unable to look at her. We were four months away from the main event, and I was mentally prepared to battle it out with my mom. I could already hear her yelling at me about how she had already paid the vendors and sent out invitations. People had already booked plane tickets from across the country. *Jesus Christ Samantha!* I imagined her screaming at me.

*Catholic?* my mom asked unruffled. She kept her eyes on the road as she spoke. Her hands didn't appear to grip the wheel harder and I didn't see signs of distress on her face. She was apparently an Oscar winning actress or she truly wanted to hear me out. I instinctively gripped my seat belt, sure she was about to shove me right out the car. Nothing happened, however, and I remained safely in my seat as she calmly explained to me that after thoughtful consideration she and my dad chose to raise my brother and I in the reformed Jewish faith, my father's religion, because they thought it was an open–minded, loving religion built around the idea of community and helping to make the world a better place. My mother grew up Southern Baptist, and she remembered it as a fearful approach to religion that she didn't want for us. While my mom appreciated many aspects of Judaism, she still maintained a soft spot for Jesus and didn't feel the need to convert herself. She infrequently attended a Methodist Church, which seemed to be a natural fit for her. Although she knew it wasn't the same as going to a Catholic service, she invited me to attend a service with her to see how it felt.

I had expected screaming, crying and threats of a lifelong grounding. This open conversation caused me to feel more stressed than I had felt before the conversation started. I had no idea anyone would actually give me a choice in the matter. *I can't make a decision like this. I'm only thirteen,* I thought. Everything had already left my mouth, however, so at this point I had to excitedly jump into the bed I had made for myself. *That sounds nice; I would love to go with you.* I said to my mom trying to sound unaffected.

We made plans to go on Wednesday night. My Christian girl gang was thrilled when I told them the news. They had already told their youth pastor about me, and I had been invited to start attending their after–school meetings and weekend events. This was working out really well socially for me. In middle school feeling comfortable around your peers is much more important than figuring out your religious identity.

Wednesday night arrived and my stomach spun

in knots on the drive to church. As we walked in, two men greeted us smiling and handed us Bibles. We found our seats and I flipped through the book. It read left to right like all the other books I owned and it read entirely in English. I watched families chat with one another and small children run around the aisles. Then, with a loud honk of the pipe organ, the service began. Everyone stood up and started to sing a song I didn't know. The entire service I lagged one beat behind everyone else. I couldn't figure out when to sit, stand, or bow my head. I felt funny saying *Jesus* out loud in a non–sarcastic manner. I stayed in my seat during Communion, moving my legs to the side to let others walk through our aisle.

Halfway through the service, I panicked. My kishkas knew I had made a mistake. None of it felt right to me. I hated not being able to sing along with any of the songs, and I didn't know the prayers. Before the service ended, I had completely zoned out. I was frantically mulling over how I could commit myself to Judaism, go to Heaven, and continue expanding my group of Christian youth group friends. Last month the youth group went on a whitewater rafting trip! I knew those summer camp brochures would come out soon and I desperately wanted in. My palms began to sweat and my stomach churned. My brain was dissolving as I couldn't figure out a way in which to have everything. I was mashugana. I didn't feel comfortable here and I suddenly wished I were trying to hold in a laugh with Emma in the back of our temple. Silence permeated the car ride home. My mom didn't push me with any questions.

Before bed I thanked my mom for taking me to church with her, and told her that I wanted to go through with my Bat Mitzvah and that I felt newly committed to Judaism. In retrospect, turning your back on Judaism before having a Bat Mitzvah is probably one of the most Jewish things a Jew can do. The stereotype of the neurotic Jew is, after all, based off millions of years of actual neurotic Jews. That night my mom gave me a big hug and sent me off to bed with the smile of a woman whose plan had worked exactly the way she hoped. I took down the quotes from my wall before going to sleep. My CGG (Christian Girl Gang) looked disappointed when I broke the new, but said they understood. They later revoked the invitation to join their youth group, and I would still not be allowed to attend coed boxcar Christian camp. For two weeks in the summer I would once again live deep in the woods in a tiny tent with no electricity or boys. While I don't know it at the time everything works out for the best. Girl Scout Camp will be one of my most cherished childhood memories, and the lack of boys will be fine, seeing as it turns out I won't like them anyways.

# ʙlack ʟight

Tim and I hung around his older sister Jackie's room poking through her CD collection and playing with her newly installed black light. The afternoon heat stifled the outside air, forcing us to forgo out usual neighborhood adventures and to find ways of killing time indoors. It was 1999, Jackie was a sophomore in high school and interested in all things grunge. She wore Nirvana T-shirts, watched every episode of MTV's *Unplugged* concerts, and one of the two local alternative radio station was all that blared from her bedroom – Tim and I thought she was the coolest. Though six years older, Jackie tolerated us more than she needed to and I couldn't get enough of her.

Luckily, Jackie didn't mind having miniature admirers around which was why she allowed us to hang out in her room for short 30-minute intervals. *Get out*, she would say, but always with a wink when one of her friends called. She easily shooed us into the hallway shutting the door right behind us moving on to something better than hanging out with 12-year-old kids. Sometimes she would let me stay and paint my nails while she chatted away on the phone to her friends. I listened intently and tried to take mental notes on the intricate workings of high school. It seemed like everyone spent the weekend wasted and making out. Although I didn't know what "wasted" meant it seemed associated with very chic parties and I looked forward to the prospect of kissing with tongues. Jackie often gave me old CDs that she had tired of, my favorites including The Cardigans' *First Band on the Moon*, and the first album that felt like an awakening slap in the face, Fiona Apple's, *Tidal*. Years later I recall reading reviews of the album and not understanding the reviewer's confusion over much of the album, especially the song "Sullen Girl." People (men) at the time debated the song and lyric, *He drove ashore and took my pearl, and left an empty shell of me.*

The first time I heard this line I was 12 and soaking in a bathtub listening to my Walkman and pretending to be my mother, which primarily involved filling the tub with bath crystals and flipping through fitness magazines. The song lyrics pierced my brain and shook me to the core. It felt like someone knew my secret. I stopped the song and replayed the lyrics no less than one hundred times. Nothing had every sounded so accurate, and I felt angry at Fiona for putting out such a shameful truth. I assume anyone else who has experienced a sexual trauma found the same revelation in the lyrics and album. Reviewers (men) debated whether Fiona was just a girl who allowed men to leave her empty or if the song was a nod to an event more sinister than being dumped. It was so painfully obvious at 12 that I couldn't believe other people (men) didn't understand.

The black light in Jackie's room was a new addition, and Tim and I couldn't get over how edgy it seemed. We put on white t–shirts, blasted the radio and shut off the lights creating our own rave in a room. The two of us danced around to Korn's *Freak on a Leash* with our glowing shirts mimicking one another's moves, and trying to maintain a serious disposition despite holding in laughs. At some point we began dancing around the bulb like ancient tribal people who had first discovered fire. I could feel the heat coming off the bulb, and it seemed much hotter than a regular light bulb. The heat transfixed me in place. I stopped dancing, facing myself directly towards the bulb, waving my hand towards it to feel the warmth.

*Be careful,* Tim said, *don't get too close to that!* He pulled me away and turned on the light.

He was always protective.

*Let's go play Mario Karts,* Tim said as he removed his white t–shirt and headed downstairs, already bored with the magic light. I remained frozen in place staring at the purple bulb and fantasizing about the heat. My brain lit up and a sudden and overwhelming thought to touch the bulb blazed into my mind. I wanted to grab it and let it sizzle on my palm. The thought of the heat on my hands made my pulse quicken and a rush surged through me. In that moment the idea of holding pain seemed like both a rational and interesting thought.

*Your dad is here,* my babysitter called up the stairs. *Time to go!*

I took off my borrowed white shirt and laid it on the bed as I walked towards the door, but before I reached the knob my brain overrode my feet and I spun around grabbing the purple light with both hands. Electricity surged through my body. The pain felt precise and awakening. My body pulsated with energy. Looking at my hands I could see them throbbing, but I felt newly alert. I felt happy. My excitement faded as I realized that my palms had ballooned up with blisters, and I would quickly need an explanation for myself. I ran to the bathroom running my hands under cool water hoping the blisters dissipated. They didn't. Within a minute they turned from pink to red and finally transformed into a dark purple. A thick piece of skin began to peel off and slip backwards, like the page of a book left out in the rain. I walked down the stairs with my hands straight out for everyone to see as it seemed like there was no point in hiding it. My dad stood in the kitchen with my little brother.

*I had an accident,* I said holding up my hands straight up as if saying, "I'm innocent." *I tripped and grabbed the lamp on my way down.* I said in a mumble. Everyone looked confused, but there wasn't much to discuss. Holding onto the tips of fingers my dad examined the blistered, and decided we should go to Urgent Care. On the drive over, he didn't press me further about the incident. He just kept asking if they hurt and telling me not to worry.

At Urgent Care the doctor inspected my hands and appeared more suspicious than the previous adults. *You fell and grabbed a light bulb?* he said with one eyebrow cocked.

*Yes.* I responded not making eye contact.

*This looks pretty severe. Are you sure?* He asked giving me another chance to fill in the obvious missing information.

*Yes. I don't know.* I said unable to form a reasonable lie. *I fell and grabbed onto it.*

After that, there was even less to say. I stuck to my story, and no one directly asked me if I did it on purpose. The doctor gave me burn cream to use for the week and wrapped my palms in gauze. *They look like mummy hands,* I said to no one in particular on the walk back to the car, trying to lighten the mood and serve as an indicator that nothing serious had taken place.

As much as I enjoyed the energy and elation from the black light, I knew grabbing light bulbs would never be a sustainable hobby. It was too obvious the first time; I knew it couldn't get away with it twice. A few months later I saw a show on National Geographic about young boys in Papua New Guinea using self–mutilation as a means to declare their manhood. It intrigued me to see an entire culture using self–harm as an acceptable ritual. While I knew the light incident wasn't about trying to convince any one of my impeding transition into adulthood, the show did allow me to feel less weird about the exciting sensation I received from burning my hands. The show gave my initial experience with self–harm a sense of belonging and a tribe of people to relate to, even if they were on the other side of the globe. Watching the Papua New Guinea boys helped me turn my impulsive act into the beginning of a personal ritual and seeing the boys cut lines into their skin also gave me an idea of self–tattooing. I would scratch a pattern into my ankle with an exacto knife that I had stolen from my art class, crack open an BIC pen, pour in the ink, and finally cover the creation with my mother's powdered concealer. Creating a tattoo on my body allowed me get the physical sensations I sought while providing some distance from actual actions I was engaging in.

By convincing myself that this was an act of art, I could hide from the fact that I enjoyed cutting open my skin. Engaging in this art allowed me to perform magic tricks with my feelings. I could make them disappear, redirect them, or create entirely new ones. Tattooing gave me the ability to momentarily escape the body in which I was becoming increasingly more uncomfortable living in. The tattooing went on for months and as a young healthy person, my skin healed quickly and absolutely. The elapsed time of tattooing to scab was 6 days and only another 3 for it to seem like I had never violently violated myself.

I talked to Katy about my new hobby and convinced her that we should make matching best friend tattoos. At first, she was all in, she grabbed a notepad and started sketching out design ideas. Once we had a design that we both agreed on she did the doodle first on her ankle then on mine. After the design pattern lay out on our ankles I went to get my exacto knife. When I arrived back I watched Katy's face transform into one obvious discomfort. *I don't want a real tattoo,* she said. *Won't that hurt? Have you done this before?* She asked making a face as if she had suddenly caught a whiff of something putrid.

Examining her wrinkled nose and judgmental eyes, I realized maybe I was doing something wrong and moving forward, I should I keep the tattooing private. *Of course not, never mind,* I said. Katy's face amplified my feelings of not being understood, alone, and apart. In that moment it became clear that she was not my tribe. I quickly grabbed the pack of gel pens and asked her what colors we should fill in the outlines with. Seeming to have already forgotten my horrifying suggestion to carve into our bodies, she chose pink and green. We filled in our ankles and admired our matching marks. Katy, our new tattoos, and I then headed out to ride our bikes to the lake. The afternoon was long and lazy in a way that afternoons can only be when you're young and don't have the need to count hours. Katy and I laid out cloud gazing, spying on Katy's crush who had a house right on the water, and debating whether or not we would be too old to go to Girl Scout camp for one last summer next year.

By the time dusk hit and we parted ways, I noticed that the sweat from the afternoon had soaked through my sock and erased my tattoo. As I rode home alone I kept replaying the uncomfortable scene from earlier. An acute shame washed over me and deepened my initial suspicion that I indeed was a bad, weird freak. Soon after this incident, the elaborate tattooing process began to feel less meaningful, and I knew I was over complicating its true purpose. Reality became impossible to ignore and I couldn't hide from the fact that digging into my skin was what most interested me, so I shifted over to this leaving the idea of body art behind.

By ninth grade I had created a fully formed ritual of cutting. I had a ziplock bag full of broken compact mirror pieces and various razor blades. While an exacto knife provided a clean slit, I more enjoyed scrapping through the layers of my skin with the glass from a compact. I liked to run one piece back and forth over the same area of skin in a way that I couldn't do with the blade for fear of cutting too deep. With each scrape, a new layer of skin would reveal itself. Each layer would get thinner and whiter until a uniformed line of dotted blood bubbled up and seeped out. My skin burned.

I would stop scraping to watch the blood escape my body and roll over spreading across the rest of my skin. Cleaning up involved patting down the wound with hydrogen peroxide while examining the rusty colored bubbles that formed. My skin ached for hours. Sometimes my leg would move a particular way and the fresh cut would sting from rubbing up against my jeans causing me to wince. The concentrated pain felt electrifying in a satisfying way, and I delighted in the knowledge of pinpointing exactly where the pain came from. At night I rubbed my scabs tenderly as they healed in the same manner I once rubbed my stuffed dog's furry ear as a child. I loved the visual of my scabs and the tactile experience of them. It felt powerful to have a secret with myself. My behavior went on like this undetected for 3 years.

**(MB as therapist)** *Why don't we call these little anxieties gremlins? Take the power from those anxieties.*
**(MB as self)** *Why don't we just call them anxieties?*
**(MB as therapist)** *Would you be more comfortable with goblins?*
**(MB as self)** *Yes.*

—*Maria Bamford*

Buddhists, the good folks at AA, or maybe Beyoncé once said you will meet your teacher only once you're ready to be taught. I've had 7 therapists in my life and I've only been ready to learn 1.5 times.

This was not one of those times.

I asked my mom to drop me off out front of the office and meet back in at the same point in exactly 60 minutes. *Do not come in,* I repeated to her slamming the car door behind me. I was furious with my parents for sending me to a therapist. Therapists were for kids with divorced parents, girls with eating disorders, and for that sexy psychopath teen in *Cruel Intentions*. I was 16, maintained a 3.6 G.P.A., participated in after school activities, was hardly sexually active, and always made it home by curfew. Maybe I engaged in cutting (and occasional binge drinking, pill popping, shoplifting, and self–loathing), but no one knew about the other stuff and in general, my life was together. Everything on the outside was going exactly how it should according to typical social norms. I didn't need therapy.

The day after my parents found out I was cutting was the most embarrassing day of my life. It felt worse than the day my dad found my vibrator while changing my bed sheets (He placed it under my pillow, even though I kept it under my mattress. We obviously never discussed the incident or made eye contact for at least 2 weeks), or the afternoon my mom confronted me about discovering the book *Same Sex in the City* tucked behind my bed (*I saw it on the Tyra Banks show! It's just a book! Don't be so close–minded about my reading choices!* I screamed defensively). The awkwardness from the cutting revelation followed me like shit–stained toilet paper stuck to my foot. The notion that everyone could see this awful truth about me was overwhelming. For days the initial conversation with my mom had been replaying in my head:

She sat on her bed crying and reached out to hug me as I entered the room. I fell into her arms knowing I could fix it. *It's not a big deal,* I said. *It's just this thing I've been doing. I can stop.*

*I don't understand. Are you sad? Did we do something wrong? What's going on?* She said through hysterical breaths. I had never seen such fear and sadness in another person, and knew I would do anything to not see that face again. I promised her I would fix everything and be good.

The next morning, I tried to stay in my room as long as possible as the thought of looking my parents in the eyes was unbearable. Eventually, I ventured down the hall to watch TV. My dad came in and asked if he could make me something to eat. *Do you want me to make you eggs and toast?* he said, barely opening the door enough to stick his head in. I knew what he this offer was supposed to convey, but I felt more embarrassed that he couldn't even say the words out loud. *Of course not,* I said keeping my eyes on the T.V. screen. To this day this exchange has been our only conversation about my self–injurious behavior.

Although I initially promised my parents I would fix everything, I never thought that agreement would mean having to seek professional help. While I wanted to make them happy, I was angry and felt like a crazy person for being 16 and having a shrink. Not understanding anything about the therapeutic process

I initially assumed I could smart my way out of it. At my first appointment I come prepared with stacks of papers highlighted and underlined referencing self–harm as a common practice in many societies. My research documented stories about young men going through self–mutilation ceremonies as right–of–passage in their communities. I circled part of an article that noted boys in Africa who would cut their skin cut so heavily and neatly that it begins to resemble that of an alligator. Other research I brought discussed how adolescent males throughout the Sudan cut parallel lines across their forehead to demonstrate to the local tribes of their impending manhood. Marks ran along the page highlighting that forehead cutting showed their village that they had fully transformed from useless little boys into brave men who could now be considered functional members of society. I had noted research on Flagellants from the 13th and 14th century who whipped themselves to the point of deep bloody gashes to absolve themselves from sin and declare their love to the Lord. Another article in my stack mentioned women flagellants engaging in similar behavior to ensure fertility. My mountain of self–harm research definitively proved that humans have been practicing and engaging in self–harm purposefully for all of recorded time from every corner of the planet. Such an array of humans couldn't be wrong about a behavior. I was fine. After all, I was just an adolescent; maybe this was my transition into adulthood.

Dr. Shayne sat smiling as I finished explaining about the flagellants of the 13th and 14th century and the global ceremonies surrounding self–mutilation and the transitional aspects of the rituals. Her smile felt annoying and patronizing. Practically out of breath from all the explaining I finally said, *Obviously this is not big deal. Can you tell my parents I'm ok?*

*Well, are you trying to show your community that you ready to take on the responsibilities of adulthood?* Dr. Shayne asked with a stupid crooked adult smile.

*No. I don't even want anyone to know that I've been doing this. Besides, I already had my Bat Mitzvah, which showed my religious community I am technically an adult.* I replied trying to sound like a smart ass. I started to bring my legs to a crisscross position on the chair with a sudden urge of wanting to become small.

*Are you repenting for your sins, or trying to show God you your commitment to him?* she asked calmly.

*No, Jews only repentant once a year during Yom Kippur,* I said and began to unconsciously bring my knees up to my chin.

*Well then, what exactly are you doing?* she asked with no hint of agenda in her voice.

*I don't know,* I said quietly. Truthfully, I wasn't entirely sure why I kept hurting myself. I had never spent much time thinking about why I kept returning to the same behavior. My eyes held steady on the tops of my shoes and I stopped speaking. Dr. Shayne didn't fill the silence. *I guess, it makes me feel…relaxed,* I said after a few mute minutes. My earlier confidence dissipated completely. *It feels good in a way I can't explain. I like it. It makes my skin calm. I don't want to die if that's what everyone is worried about,* I said.

We talked a while longer and for a moment the talking felt nice, but then Dr. Shayne asked, *Have you ever been sexually abused or assaulted?*

*No, no that never happened to me* I said stammering, breaking eye contact, and looking at the multitude of thick psychology books on her shelf.

After the session ended I met my mom in the exact place she dropped me off, and we drove home with not one word spoken between us. Lying in bed that night I wished I could go back and redo the entire session. I wanted to go back into Dr. Shayne's office and tell her everything; the boy, his hands on me, my panic, the frequency of his hands on me, how I hated touching him, the smell, not knowing when it would happen next, the feelings of being chosen and special and repulsive, and how sometimes I wanted to rip all my skin off. I didn't want to hold this heavy secret any longer. Dr. Shayne would never ask me outright again, and I never could muster the courage to bring it up on my own.

After a handful of sessions passed, I felt like I had missed my opportunity completely, but figured at least one of us should feel successful so I spent the next 12 weeks lying and pretending to get better. It was very clear that my time with Dr. Shayne was on an insurance deadline, and I couldn't stomach the thought of leaving my last session without everyone feeling like I was good, better, healed. Moments arose when Dr. Shayne would look at me sincerely or a make a face indicating she cared and for a second I wanted to try honestly explaining myself, but I couldn't. The words to describe my sexual assault were physically stuck in my throat. I literally couldn't produce even the most basic language to outline what happened to me. I certainly didn't have the language to articulate the overwhelming compulsion I had or how my skin felt itchy and like cutting it open was the only way to get the itching to stop. At the time I couldn't articulate that my skin sometimes felt two sizes too small and how occasionally it might feel like bugs were crawling in–between my bones and tendons. Getting rid of these feelings was the only thing that made sense, but I couldn't figure out how to speak about that either. It seemed from the lack of conversation with my parents, post–therapy sessions and in general about my cutting that they didn't have the words to talk about it either. Pick up, drop off, talk about dinner options, finish your homework, and repeat.

My need to do well kept me showing up to sessions and trying to reassure everyone around me that things were *fine*. By the time the final session arrived, I had convinced myself that something was in fact deeply wrong with me, but I could just go on forever hiding in my own witness protection program. I wasn't that boy on an island with a tribe full of others who understood him, and I would have to balance my two cracked selves alone:

"I'm journaling, I'm listening to music, I'm following through with my relaxation plan. Thanks for everything Dr. Shayne, I feel much better."

# Translations

E ven as small children, girls have an innate sense to write, particularly about their internal on–goings. It was during a weekend in L.A. when my grandparents babysat me while my own folks spent time adulting in Las Vegas that my grandma gifted me my first journal. The outside was textured in black cotton full of small red roses with dark green stems. This journal had previously belonged to my aunt which made it all the more special since at the time she was the most radical woman I knew. At five I couldn't write simple sentences without help, but I immediately enjoyed having a space to fill. Every afternoon before dinner I would write one sentence with the help of my grandma, and then draw in an accompany picture for the full visual effect. Grandpa and me play video games. *Grandpa and me ride a motorcycle* (\*moped). The act of creating my own narrative stuck, thus beginning my compulsive need to fill pages. In the early thick of my written expressive purging I didn't overthink the idea of "Dear journal" or even wonder who was this "journal" that I sending my inner dialogue to. Up until fourth grade I started or ended each entry with a formal acknowledgement of the journal (Dear Journal and Bye Journal). As I aged this formality started feeling silly and childlike, although this didn't completely stop me from writing BYE! at the completion of each account. The correspondence aspect continues to make me wonder who are dispatching our reflections to; a higher version of ourselves, a best friend, a cosmic feminine energy source that girls have been contributing to since the dawn of time?

Reexamining my journals illuminates a clear path of my history of self–deception. My lying was never the over–the–top, attention–seeking kind – except in third grade I announced to my class that Mariah Carey was my aunt, in fifth grade I nonchalantly mentioned to my class I fluently read and wrote Hebrew, and in the same year, my best friend and I constantly acted out elaborate fight scenes in order to get sent to the guidance office during class time. The majority of lying in my journal took the form of self–preservation. Multiple little lies helped to craft a truth that was more easily digestible to me. Delusional is too big of a word as my deceits usually danced around some version of the truth.

Writing and believing in my fiction was survival. It provided a way in which to hide myself from myself. However, the "Hitler wisdom" of lying long enough and loud enough eventually making something true never fully work on me, despite my best efforts. I vividly recall fabricating ideas about myself while simultaneously jamming down and shoving over any kernels that felt too authentic. All the energy I spent attempting to build my own version of truth proved futile because although I couldn't stand my genuine self, I couldn't wholly embrace the fable of my creation. Some people are more skilled in this than others.

Here is a truthful translation of my journal entries which sadly prove my deep need for self–avoidance even in the place that was supposed to be private and nonjudgmental.

*December 2, 1997*

*GAY*

*Today I found out that uncle adam is GAY. Dad told me. O'h Lord he's gay. So that's why he sleep node (nude) with ken. He loves Ken. I feel weird now. I can not belive (believe) that. But I still love him. By Joral (Journal) PS. O'h Lord*

*\*Accompanying picture of my uncles kissing.*

At age eight I think my spelling could have been better, and my sentence structure is clearly appalling. These literary transgressions are likely proof of my slight familial history of dyslexia (*How do you spell "BECAUSE"* my mom would yell from the computer in our living room. *REALLY DAWN* my dad would yell back before spelling it aloud).

The amount of "Oh Lord's" seen in this entry leads me to believe I am more Southern than I like to admit or that I've always had the internal dialogue of a drag queen. This entry is a rare example of an honest reaction to an experience, which I attribute to age. Learning to hide your true self comes from watching the world react to you through time, and I didn't have too much of that under my belt yet. The news of my uncle's gayness floored me; it was the equivalent shock of learning Santa isn't real. My tiny brain could hardly wrap itself around the idea especially since in 1997 gayness wasn't as visible as it is today. This early entry makes me feel proud (and embarrassed from a writing point of view) because it's an example of watching my younger self work through a societal challenge and ultimately decide to accept my uncle out of love. Love overpowered any inkling I had that being gay was "bad."

Thinking back, I actually spent a significant amount of time with two lesbians at my babysitter's house growing up, Diane and Diane. They would come over and do arts and crafts with us, show us how to garden, and read us Eric Carle stories. In the afternoon they could be found walking around the neighborhood together in similar windbreakers with coordinating pants. Lying does take place in this entry in the form of my one added unnecessary sentence: *so that's why he sleeps nude with Ken.* I was never privy to their sleeping situation and can't say why I added such a personal detail.

*November 12, 2003*

*Hillary is my best friend. I have best friends at school that I've had for years but this is different. We talk about all the important stuff. She's sad like me too sometimes. I dont have any friends that are sad. Everyone at school is always happy and talking about boys that they make out with and parties they go to. I can talk to her on the phone for hours. Maybe it's because she's older. She's already senior! She's much smarter than me, but I think she likes me as much as I like her. She's older but hasn't done that many things (maybe nothing!) with guys. I can spend more time with her than anybody else. We have sooo much to talk about it. I think she worries about me sometimes. Shes the first person I've told about some of my "stuff." I dont like her worrying about me, but I like that she cares about me so much. I already hate thinking about her going to college next year. It will probably be out of state and she'll forget about me when she makes new friends and starts being an adult.*

Here is an example of well–intended self–deception. Writing this one entry took longer than usual because I had to constantly stop my stream of consciousness and choose my words carefully as to not it make it sound as if I had deep romantic feelings for Hillary, which I did. By the time I reached my teenage years, I didn't feel like my journal was a safe and private space although I had no reason to think otherwise. My parents never read it and in fact, they were pro–privacy for my writing. Trusting myself with myself felt impossible. By the time I had written this post I had already fantasized what kissing Hillary would feel like and I frequently thought about women when I masturbated; mainly teachers, coaches, Alice from *The L Word*, and Julianne Moore specifically from *Boogie Nights*. As high school went on, I started censoring my masturbation fantasies and forcing myself to think of the popular, cute, age appropriate guys in my grade. I grieve for all those wasted orgasms.

My 15–year–old self knew my feelings surrounding Hillary were complex, but I was terrified about the idea of being with her. My friends at school were all femme girls obsessed with typical boys, and everyone in my high school used "dyke" and "fag" as casual slurs. Hillary and I spent the majority of our time together passionately debating anything and everything, worrying about one another, and talking about how miserable we were (ie; watching *The Hours* repetitively and listening to emo music on long car rides). Deep down our relationship felt like my first real romantic relationship, emotionally. Essentially, we conducted ourselves as a young couple that was saving themselves for marriage.

While our relationship felt emotionally serious, I constantly fought hard against even thinking about it having a physical part. If we had a sleepover we did sleep, squished against each other in a way that felt romantic. Despite all of this, my brain couldn't entirely imagine the totality of a relationship with her. It just wasn't something anyone my age dabbled in publicly, and I desperately wanted to be normal. The lack of emotional depth blares in this entry. The simple concrete sentences appear more like how an elementary school student would write than a hormonal teen. My inability to emote is apparent and derived from a fear of outing myself to myself. The lack of passion in this entry completely contradicted my saccharine self at the time. I worked tirelessly to keep these feelings off the pages. At the very least, I did carry the awareness that I craved her complete attention and affection.

*August 16, 2005*

*So I had sex w/Mark\* today!! O–M–Fucking goodness! I thought about it all day long today during band camp. I cant really believe I did it! We were at my house at first, and then he didn't have a condom, we went to Walgreens, then to his house. At first it hurt, a lot, but then all the sudden it just felt really good. Sadly, it was probably only 3.5 minutes. It was different than I thought, but I can see how after lots of practice it'd be awesome. I think, however, I almost get off more when he fingers me. I dunno, it was good. Im sad hes leaving because now I want to do it again! Hahaha! Meredith\* gave me a big hug because she was so proud. Its weird too, just because its not how I imagined it all going. Im glad though, Im gonna be a senior this year, its about time! OOO la la! I need to go call Jennifer and Lauren!*

This is self–preservation lying mixed with a hopeful projection of how I wish I'd felt. The basic run down of deflowering scene is honest. It was my idea to have sex. Mark did look shocked when I suggested it, and I did accompany him into Walgreens. I even offered to pay for the condoms (this is what girls raised on Spice Girls, Destiny's Child, and Janet Jackson grow up to do. Cue: Independent Women Throw Your Hands Up At Me). His mom cooked dinner upstairs while we engaged in underage sex in the basement. The basement was musty and, luckily, dark. The entirety of the room was covered in cat hair and dust. My skin always itched after spending time down there. Mark acted as the expert on sex even though he had only had sex with one other girl, and it occurred when he was wasted at a party two years prior.

Mark asked me if I was ready and kissed my forehead in way that made me uncomfortable and my stomach turn. This act of masculinity made me squeamish and unattached although I realize straight women might have interpreted these actions as sweet and comforting. These internal discomfort signals should have been a big clue that I was indeed a lesbian, but I was committed to mind over matter. Following through on this act was one of a million ways I silenced my intuition and stopped trusting myself. Ron White's low voice grumbled in the background, and I kept hearing the last bit of his joke, which sent me into a fit of giggles. The ice clinking in his glass and audience laughter were welcome distracters. During the actual sex, I grabbed the shelf behind me like I had seen René Zellweger do in *Chicago* when she was passionately cheating on her husband; I'm nothing if not committed to a role of my own creation. His forehead lined with sweat beads, which appeared odd seeing as it lasted less than 60 seconds. Maybe the room was hot; I don't remember.

Afterwards, I didn't feel any closer to him; in truth, I felt more estranged. An overwhelming sense of pride and adultness that had little to do with him and more to do with the idea of being transformed into a woman was the only positive emotion I gained. I wanted to have more sex with him for practice, but I didn't want to see him at college or have him come home to visit me. No primal urge to marry him or even call him my boyfriend seeped into me. When lying to my friends about the historic event I told them the sex had made me crazy about him because I thought it was the right thing to say. My acting skills progressed and I would get drunk after he left for college and cry to my friends about missing him. A few times I thought maybe the sex did make me love him, but my body would check me afterwards when he would try to cuddle up next me causing me to twitch like someone poked me in the side with a sizzling cattle prod. Usually I would get up and leave moments after it ended. *I'll be outside* I would say taking his cigarettes. Even though I just held the smoke in my mouth and puffed it out, I enjoyed the ritual. It added to feeling adult, cool, and unattached and, it was a great excuse to leave.

I stopped keeping a journal once college started. The act felt immature, but also futile, as it didn't seem useful to write a book full of known lies, which at that point was all my entries would have been. My thoughts and feelings felt too overwhelming to record. Certainly, I couldn't write about the idea that maybe I didn't like boys the way I was supposed to, or how I hated my body, thought I was a slut, or jot down notes regarding preoccupation with self harm in various forms. Most of all, I couldn't write down my biggest worry, that I had long held the nagging sense that I might not make it to 30. Nothing was left to write about, so I dropped my old hobby and trapped these thoughts and feelings in my mind with nowhere to go. They started to sit, ruminate, and rot me from the inside out, which is what happens when you don't let living things have fresh air or allow them any natural light.

Journaling was for girls with age appropriate heterosexual crushes who dreamed about candlelight dates and holding hands. Journaling was for girls who cared about prom and wrote with feminine curly letters, carefully places hearts over their "I's" and owned matching pen sets. That girl wasn't me, and I had a suspicion it would best for everyone if my thoughts remain locked inside for no one to see.

# Babysitters Club

To all the families that I babysat for between the ages of 13–16,

I'm sorry. I was an irresponsible thief of a babysitter. I stole, broke things, kissed boys in your homes, and lied. I'm sorry. I began with good intentions. Your kids were cute, and I thought since I was an older sister and a Girl Scout, I already contained all the necessary perquisites to be a successful sitter. This combination caused many of you to also believe that I was innately responsible. Being in your homes, however, was too much freedom for me. Too many things to snack on, snoop through, and take.

I'd like to send a general sorry to all the families for eating all of your snacks. It started off as it innocently enough, as it does for all babysitters, with raiding your family's food. To be fair, you guys did offer the food in your homes up to me. I was often told with gusto by the dads to enjoy anything in the fridge and pantry. *Help yourself to anything you want*, they said. I had no guilt about rifling through your cabinets and refrigerator looking for snacks better than, or at least different, from the ones in my home.

At first I enjoyed novelty children's treats such as Rice Krispie Treats and rainbow–colored Goldfish. While I didn't care for the way they stuck to my back molars, I loved the squirt of a fresh Gusher and found myself eating at least half the box. Within 10 minutes, my mouth would be stained purple from the mix of the flavors and my teeth half an inch bigger covered with the sticky gooey treat. Soon, however, I became bored with fruit roll–up and fun–sized candy bars. My palette has always prefers savory to sweet. This boredom caused me to engage in a little more looking, and I realized for the first time that adults had their own versions of treats. My focus switched to these new adult treats. I prided myself on being able to climb up tall cabinets, silent ninja style, and use my one free arm as a seeing eye to locate boxes of grown–up crackers and olive jars that were most likely being saved for company. In my defense, you never explicitly stated not to eat those. I sifted through the fridge moving past the Oscar Mayer bologna slices (though I always rolled one up into a proper log form and munched on it before moving past it) in order to find that good adult meat: prosciutto, hard salamis, soft salamis, at least some cubed ham pieces. The fancy mustard always hid behind the yellow one, saved for children without experienced taste buds.

I laid out all my ingredients on the kitchen island in order of use– crackers, mustard, good adult meat, and any cheese that came in a hunk form. It wasn't exactly an assembly line– I preferred doing each task in its entirety.

First I would lie out six crackers (years of research has proven this to be the perfect snack number; double for an entire meal), dab a medium sized mustard blob on each cracker. You don't want too much mustard because this will overpower the other flavors, but not enough mustard will leave with you with a dry mouth.

Next came folding and placing a piece of meat on top of each cracker. Obviously since salami is already perfectly circled, it was easy to just place this directly on top matching circle to circle (unless, of course, your crackers are squares and rectangles, in such case, just center it the best you can).

Slicing the cheese was my favorite part– I cut a slice to place on top of the meat and then I cut a thinner slice to pop right into my mouth. This stacking and popping continued in a rhythmic fashion until each cracker had all necessary accruements.

Then, I would put all the ingredients away allowing myself to admire my perfectly portioned, delicious creations before eating them all one by one. With the crackers, of course, I would need eat half a container of the nine dollar olives I had found and wash it down with a bottle of sparkling water in your house, if you had it. If not, I would drink the most expensive liquid I could find which was typically a Snapple or Fresca.

Essentially– if you give a teen a pantry she'll want something to eat. I stand by the idea that this wasn't considered stealing since technically you said I could.

I apologize specifically to the Jones family. I started babysitting for you around 15, which was the same age I realized houses contained fun adult items that I might want to take home with me, or at least hold and examine. Mrs. Jones, you did repeatedly tell me to make myself at home, which is the English translation of *mi casa es su casa*, which as I understand it culturally means *have anything of mine you want*. I'm sorry I went through your bedside tables and underwear drawers looking for sex toys. I did found a whole drawer of vibrators, handcuffs, soft porn DVDs, and the pièce de résistance, a purple double–sided dildo. I laughed as soon as I came across it thinking about your husband using this one in particular. He operated primarily on overt masculinity and toughness. He was a hard–ass with your sons and more than once I saw him give them high fives as they went in for a hug. Even if he didn't use this himself I knew he must be more open–minded than he appeared to allow this wide array of colorful toys in your bedroom. He must also be sweeter than he presents seeing as your porn collection consisted of a DVD with titles like "sexy beach party house" and "make love to me in Paris." Maybe you guys were swingers; that would make more sense for that particular toy anyways which to my limited knowledge is used primarily between two women. Don't worry, I didn't take, or use any of your sex gear. I just liked to see them and hold them up close. I couldn't find equipment that serious at the Spencer's at our mall. Actually now that I'm thinking about it, I might have used one of the pocket vibrators while sitting on the edge of your bathtub with my bare feet pressed against the cold tile floors. It was the kind of vibrator that if you saw in a junk drawer you might think it was a container to hold lipstick or some sort tiny Tupperware for gherkins. If it makes you feel better I swear I used it over my pants, scouts honor, no skin to toy contact. And I never ever used anything that required insertion.

I would like to send a huge sorry to the Smith family who had the best–filled bathroom cabinets on our street, and I took an ordinate amount of pills from it. From my investigation, it appeared Mr. Smith had raging hemorrhoids as apparent by the tubs of Preparation–H under the sink on his side of the double vanity. This was a prewipes era; all dads had were tubs of white paste to manually tack on their butts. It seemed like everyone in your home had allergies since I found Allegra in every drawer of your house, though this was no interest to me. It also appeared like you guys could not sleep to save your lives. The Smith's bathroom cabinet ranged from Tylenol PM Cold to Ambien and everything in–between, including lavender sprays and chewable orange flavored melatonin. I always left with 2–4 Ambien depending on the fullness of the bottle.

I first discovered Ambien spending time with my grandparents. They lived in California and for many summers my brother and I would stay with them for a couple of weeks at a time without our parents. My grandfather had an enormous size bottle of Ambien that frankly didn't look legal – I'm talking protein powder size tub. Everyone went to sleep relatively early so I would get bored and take one. Then I realized it would be more fun to take one and wash it down with a glass of Hpnotiq. My grandfather was not a drinker and my grandmother only drank pink wine at the time, so I was never sure why he had Hpnotiq in the house. I would take the pill and then sip and chat with all my friends on the East Coast on AIM. I would have no idea what I was typing but frequently woke up the next morning with texts saying: *you were hilarious last night, glad you're having so much fun in LA, I would love to come out and visit, do you really think your grandparents wouldn't mind?!*

My favorite Ambien game to play, however, was STAY AWAKE! I would hold out past the sleepiness, and then put on my headphones and dance around quietly in my room to Jimmy Hendrix or The Mamas and the Papas feeling very groovy all while my grandparents slept two doors down. Staying awake on Ambien is the closest I've ever been to doing a psychedelic drug. Ambien was nice, but felt best when used quietly in California.

I preferred Xanax and Valium, and the Smiths were the family who had it. It struck me odd that this was the couple that had the hard stuff because neither of the Smiths seemed overly neurotic or stressed. They seemed to take the chaos of parenting in stride, but maybe this was their secret ingredient. I always took two to four of these as well, again depending on the fullness of the bottle. One evening when I was sorting through Mrs. Smith's bedside table trying to see if she had any interesting sexy stuff, I stumbled on an entire packet of Valium covered in Hebrew writing. Their pills always lived in their cabinets. It felt out of place on top of the fact that the Smiths were not Jewish. I had never seen pills in a package form like this one. It looked like a packet that teeth whitening gum comes in. Two sheets fit nicely into one rectangular packet. I slid out a single sheet and popped out a pill just like a piece of gum.

The snap from pushing one pill out was loud and

I instinctively looked around to see if anyone heard. It quickly dawned on me that taking one pill out of an entire packet might be obvious. In a bottle no one is keeping close count; everything is scrambled up together at the bottom. I worried that they would find out and I would be fired and then everyone would know what a psycho I was and I would have no more babysitting gigs. I rubbed the package back and forth on my palm trying to figure out a way to fix it. I realized I couldn't put the pill back in; the seal was broken. It dawned on me that since I couldn't fix it I should just take the entire package. If the entire package was gone Mrs. Smith would just think *she* lost it. She would never imagine her sweet, 15–year–old, still Girl Scout–of–a–babysitter would have stolen it. That idea was too asinine to even consider. I quickly calmed down. Anyway, I knew she must have bought those pills from a hardly legal online pharmacy; it's not like I took her inhaler or her son's EpiPen, I reasoned with myself.

To the Brown family, I am sorry for watching porn on your family computer, and then not clearing the search history. You guys had the fastest dial–up on the block, but I unfortunately didn't learn that search history or the clearing of it was even a thing until I was 20. Seeing as my searchers were often items like "women kissing," "women kissing topless," "women kissing other women naked," you most likely blamed your sweet husband. While I'm sure these weren't as sophisticated as the disgusting searches your husband typically typed in, I doubt you had anyone else to blame. Sorry, Mr. Brown! I might have also given your computer a virus trying to download the Paris Hilton sex tape– I was curious! Once the crash screen popped up, I used my best technology knowledge and just held down the power button to force it asleep and walked away. Maybe when you guys turned it back on the machine nicely rebooted without problem, like most computers infected with viruses did in the early millennium.

Another apology goes out to the cool rich family that moved into our suburban neighborhood when I was in high school. I can't remember your names, but I thought you guys were uber glamorous and would have been better suited living in DC or Brooklyn. All the moms in our neighborhood dressed like… moms, and Mrs. Urbanite looked like a hip women from a *Real Housewives* franchise. She was an architect, and the inside of their house reminded me of a Restoration Hardware catalog. As kids my brother and I loved Restoration Hardware. We didn't get one at our mall until I was 12 and he was 6. We walked around touching everything. *Ohhhh that feels so nice*, my brother said moving his hand over a $6,000 petrified wooden kitchen table. *Feel these bed sheets*, I said smoothing out the silk on the display bed. We would run around the store trying to find the most expensive and smallest item. Once it was a 4–pound globe with a bronze handle that came in at $600.00. Another time it was a $150 soap container made out of steel shaped like a Trapezoid.

Family Urbanite also had a bookshelf full of binders that held hundred and hundreds of CDs. They probably had 25–30 of these CD binders that I loved thumbing through while drinking their San Pellegrino and picking out all the cashews from their nut mix. I ended up taking between 12–15 CDs, not entire binders! I assumed all your music had been downloaded/uploaded/bought on your iTunes account by that point since you all were so modern. Most people only kept CDs at that point just in case all these Internet sites and Apple technologies didn't work out, even though it was rapidly proving us otherwise. I knew I shouldn't have taken them, but some of those stolen albums saved my sanity. I listened to Nirvana's *In Utero* almost every day my junior year and Janet Jackson's *Velvet Rope* aided in my own sexual awakening. I'm shit and I'm sorry.

Shout out sorry to the McDuggar family for the time I accidently broke your washing machine. It stopped working half through a load that only included a little boy's white T–shirt tainted with a chocolate syrup stain. I know you said no ice cream, but you had three boys between the ages of 4 and 10 and in a group they scared me and I felt out of control with them. I wanted them to like me, but mostly I wanted them to not kill me. One afternoon your eldest, Scott, chased me around your house with a carving knife then proceeded to lock himself inside a closet threatening to stab a hole in a hand. I look back at this as the beginning of my crisis intervention training. I thought I loaded the machine properly, I had watched my parents do it a thousand times, but something went wrong and all of a sudden as we sat eating sprinkles out the bottle we all heard a loud clunk and the repetitive motion of the machine stopped. The boys helped me scoop out all of the water with buckets. I told them we were pirates and our boat was sinking which caused them to work hard and fast. Little Mark's forehead broke into a sweat as he waddled with the water pail from the laundry room to dumping it out on your back porch. I promised them all more ice cream for participating in the cover up. Once the water was out, I took out the shirt and threw it in the bottom of the neighbors garbage can. When the ordeal ended I learned two very important things: 1. Ice cream and secret treats always outside. 2. Just throw it out. Making something disappear is the best option.

Everyone, I am sorry! But if it makes you feel any better I was also a great sitter with your kids. While most babysitters sat around and watched TV or talked to their friends on the phone, I spent the pre–bedtime hours with your kids in interactive play. No electronics, except for the occasional Mario Kart competition. We did tons of faux science experiments where we would try to burn up ants with magnifying glasses, measure the time it took for a slug to die from pouring salt on it, and see what time of soil made the sturdiest mud castle. I taught your kids how to play Sardines and flashlight tag. I made up a wildly popular game called *mix-this-drink–that* where we would take turns choosing four items from the fridge to mix up and then for each other to take a sip. Anyone who could swallow a sip without spitting it out would make it the sudden death round where each final contestant would concoct their own drink with two ingredients and we would vote on who combined the most vile cocktail. Whoever could take the most sips of the winning drink was crowned the ultimate winner. In the summer we created homemade Slip N Slides and made bubbles from dish soap and warm water. I taught your kids how to create bubble wands by twisting wire hangers in various shaped. I played approximately 100 hours of UNO even though I never figured out the appeal of the game. Before bed I let your kids watch *The Simpsons*, *South Park*, or any scary movie that played on Showtime. We always pushed bedtime back by at least half an hour. I got them to brush their teeth and wash their faces. We always read books before bed. I squeezed your kids tight and tucked them in like little tiny burritos. I loved your kids. I guess I was innately responsible and ready for the job, but also a minor perverted, hungry criminal. I'm sorry.

# My Space

As a preteen in the early millennium, I had unfettered access to TV and internet in a way kids today could never imagine. Parental safeguards were a few years off and, like many of my peers, I was adapting to technology faster than my parents. This lack of safeguards allowed me to explore ideas surrounding sex and gave sexuality a more nuanced meaning aside from the typical labels of *straight*, *gay*, or *bi*. Saturday nights I secretly watched HBO's *Real Sex* using the television set in my family's recreational room with the door shut and the volume turned down to hardly a whisper. Sitting too close to the screen, I watched women compete in strip club pageants, couples attend tantric workshops, and learned about the complex world of BDSM all the while feeling the gamut of human emotions ranging from disgust to arousal. I never knew if I should masturbate or take notes.

The people participating in the *Real Sex* documentary were so human and unattractive that at times I had difficulty watching them partake in the array of sexual activities. Like all good Americans, I only wanted to watch beautiful super humans engaging in diverse sexual acts. *Real Sex* provided a crash course of sex positive knowledge and equipped me with a sense that no sexual act was too perverse if you could find a consenting partner. In the typical puritanical suburb that I lived in, this was a revolutionary notion. Although radical at the time, with the depth and breadth of porn available today, *Real Sex* now looks like a middle school sex education curriculum. I doubt my younger brother, or anyone a decade younger than me, would find this show anything other than humorous and retro.

While TV was the place to watch and learn, the internet was a place to practice. When the MTV show *Catfish* first aired, I couldn't believe how upset people felt over an online deception. Their genuine surprise looked naive and scripted to me. Even at thirteen, I understood that the internet had been invented for lying about ourselves, watching porn, and shopping. I knew not to trust anyone online due the fact that all my friends and I were "catfishing" everyone all the time. Emma and I spent entire Friday nights huddled around her computer laughing our asses off thinking of disgusting things to write in chat rooms. Emma's computer was in her bedroom, which only made it that much easier for us to spend extended hours of interrupted time sexting with anyone's attention we could get. We collected dick pics and examined the intricacies of the male body. In cyberspace we could experiment with language, sexual dynamics, and our bodies. I engaged in cybersex under the assumption that the person on the other line was likely not whom they presented as either, but that was the adventure.

In chat rooms we were all playing and learning. Most chat rooms in 2001 were likely filled with 13–year–old horny kids.

When interacting with strangers online my default A/S/L was 17/F/CA. At the time, seventeen sounded like the most adult age I could possible pretend to be, and California was the only glamorous state I had spent a significant amount of time in. Other days I was happy to be a 16/M/FL seeking out the sensation of participating in sexual activities as the opposite gender. I also had a sense that perverted things were happening online in swampy regions in Florida (later the show *To Catch a Predator* will prove this hunch largely true). Chat rooms provided a place to experiment with gender, sexuality, and fantasy. We are so limited by the skin in which we exist, but in this space, I could act out all the lives I ever wanted, and find the courage to begin coming to terms with my truest sexual self.

In early 2006, Facebook could only be accessed with a college email address, so while I waited patiently for my acceptance letters to arrive, Myspace was the only important online social space I could participate in. Myspace had a search option with multiple filters that I used daily, despite having the same people show up in the results section. Bisexual women between 15–25 who lived in a 25–mile radius and derived from any race and any body type were my secret filters. At the time, even thinking about checking the lesbian box filled with me more anxiety than I could digest. Culturally, bisexuals were on the edge of trendy, and this label still included the traditional idea of being interested in guys, which made me feel more normal. For a time, I chatted with a 20–year–old college student who almost exclusively wrote to me about what types of sexual situations she wanted to have me in. Her language was aggressive and detailed. Often, she referenced wanting to finger bang me in public spaces. I wasn't always entirely sure what everything meant, but I found all of her words deeply arousing. While I sought to be in romantic proximity to another girl, I felt unsure about actually partaking in anything physical. I just wanted to feel what it was like to be around a girl in a knowingly gay situation. Although I knew I was too green to meet this seasoned college student in real life, I liked fantasizing about the dirty scenarios she wrote to me.

A few weeks later, a new girl popped up on my filtered search. Chelsea was a femme bisexual girl who attended my rival high school, which was a fact neither one of could pretend to care about. She described herself as artsy and lonely, and she would email me pictures of her paintings. We never wrote to one another about anything remotely sexual. While Chelsea seemed shy, she stood comfortably in her sense of sexual self and label of bisexual. After school she worked at the Girl Scout store just a few miles away from my house. I wrote to her that I had spent countless hours in that exact store as kid. In my correspondence I included details about how my mom had been my troop leader and that my troop stayed together until my sophomore year of high school so we could all get our Silver Award together. I went on to add details about spending multiple summers at Girl Scout camp and joked how that was likely responsible for my lesbian tendencies. These are objectively embarrassing facts, but at the time I thought they might impress her. She responded saying she was also a Girl Scout for too long also, and that working at the store was a great gig because she could get high on the job and work on her sketches. Aside from being old Girl Scouts and watching *The L Word*, Chelsea and I didn't have much in common. Despite this, talking to her felt safe and exciting. I secretly hoped we would fall in love.

Two weeks after we started emailing we set up a day to meet in person and jointly considered the outing a date. While I had a boyfriend at the time, this action didn't register as cheating because I wasn't sure I would ever allow this scenario to become my real life. The day of date, I hunted through my clothes deciding if I should try looking super femme or slightly toy boyish. After trying on multiple outfits, I decided best to go as myself, which was a decision I hardly ever made when dating. Driving to the Girl Scout store, I wondered if I was automatically the boy in our relationship since I was technically picking her up. I wondered if we would kiss.

Walking into the store my stomach fluttered furiously with nerves and excitement. These butterflies disappeared upon seeing her, however – she looked different than her pictures and my imagination. My imagination had pictured her body and style differently than she presented, and I knew I didn't feel physically attracted to her. As we walked to my car, my eyes darted everywhere checking to see if I knew anyone. We quietly drove to the neighborhood lake, which was a cool place for kids to drink, smoke, make out, and hang out. Chelsea reeked of Pachulia oils and mothballs. I sent up prayer that no one I knew would be at the lake and wondered why I even considered such a public place.

As we walked around the perimeter of the lake, Chelsea talked about an ex–girlfriend and confided she still had feelings for her. My brain could hardly register her words; I was beyond impressed that she had already been in actual same sex relationship. I wanted to ask her about kissing a girl and what it felt like to have been in love, but I also wanted to appear well–versed on lesbian culture and experiences so I kept these thoughts to myself. Pauses of silence that seemed to last forever stretched out between our attempt at small talk. We spoke to another as if we were on an interview. The experience felt both unnatural and thrilling. Nothing about her caused even a flicker of arousal in me, and I knew I would never see again, but being on a bad date with a girl felt more right and comfortable than the best date I had with a guy. My typical sense of "shoulds" and "woulds" stayed at bay. When dating guys, I felt the pull of an invisible noose tightening around me the longer I stayed with them. Every time I had a boyfriend, my automatic feeling was that of being trapped. Playing the part of girlfriend to boyfriend was becoming exhausting. As I got older, this role required more elaborate convictions. For someone never formally trained as an actor, I could muster a convincing performance as straight–doting girlfriend when needed. Part of me knew that dating guys didn't feel right, however, the perception of normalcy overrode accepting my true identity and wants.

After our anticlimactic, sparkless date, I drove

Chelsea back to the Girl Scout Store. I opened her car door and walked her to the storefront overcome by the new idea that I was now a femme gentleman. We awkwardly hugged and even though I hadn't fallen in love with her, I left feeling elated. Driving home I knew I wouldn't go on anymore online dates, at least not for the time being, but I was happy to have this experience on the back burner promising myself that I would find a way back to this feeling. This tiny date will go on to sustain me during the following years as I continue to struggle with moments of pretending with guys, not allowing myself to live as my truest sexual self. College was months away, and I knew lots of same sex kissing was taking place in drunk–dark basements on campuses across the country. I would be there soon enough, I reasoned with myself. In the meantime, I knew I had the TV and internet as safe places to explore and get off.

# Buzzed

I've long appreciated feeling anything different than myself, altered and under the influence. As a young girl with no knowledge of drugs or alcohol, I was fascinated with *Alice in Wonderland*. The idea of ingesting a mysterious vial and then gaining shapeshifting powers to see the world from a new angle appealed to me. At home I would stand towering over rows of seated Barbie dolls performing as a gigantic pop super star. During games of hide and seek, I would will my body into cramped spaces under bathroom sinks or forcefully wedge it between filing cabinets, always impressed with my ability to contort. I liked playing pretend and feeling like someone else. Eventually, I'll discover actual potions of transformation, first inside of a neighbor's lukewarm wine cooler and then in parent's medicine cabinet that housed muscle relaxers and anti–anxiety treats. I'll spend time alone in my room high on whatever I can get my hands on doodling, listening to music, and enjoying the alternate reality.

Being intoxicated is a fine line of taking pleasure in various altered sensations and being more comfortable living outside of yourself as an act of avoidance. Often times these feelings and ideas overlapped for me, and I quickly realized I wasn't sure what side of the equation I sought most. As a teen I'll take Xanax and cruise the pages of Myspace examining the profiles of local bisexual and lesbian teens brave enough to put their labels online. The Xanax took enough of the edge off that I could fantasize about touching soft skin and rubbing my fingers through long hair. Things that alter have a way of exacerbating natural tendencies like lust and shame. Using illuminates conditions we're already drenched in but don't want to see. Substances fueled my curiosity and strengthened my ability to boldly flirt with girls online in high school. While under the influence I felt certain about my true sexual identify, but in the sober moments of the day I hid behind a guise of pretending it was all just a drunk or high thing I sometimes did.

Surprisingly, the first time I kissed a girl I was sober. Maybe not as surprisingly, the first time I kissed a girl it happened in with my best friend and roommate Meredith at a frat house during the first semester of my freshman year at college. Technically, Meredith and I met in second grade. There's a suburban legend she wore the same outfit as my best friend Katy and I, causing us to tease and ignore her for the rest of the school year. My junior year of high school we became instant best friends and had the sort of all–consuming female friendship you can only have in high school and college. She was the Marissa to my Summer, the Serena to my Blair, and the Meredith Grey to my Christina Yang, which is to say she was more popular, had boys constantly falling over her, and generally was more well–liked than me. Not going to college together wasn't even considered our senior year; we did all of our campus tours together and made decisions like conjoined twins. By the grace of the housing gods, we ended up as each other's "random roommate," although I've always wondered if she secretly wrote my name in on the slip of paper we sent in with our acceptance letters.

That first semester Meredith and I routinely pre–gamed at a frat house that we wouldn't be caught dead in just one year later. The guys who inhabited the house were a hodgepodge of virgins, exchange students, and hacker types. They had an outdoor space decked out with multiple beer pong tables, corn hole, but most importantly to us, they consistently had a keg in which beer flowed endlessly. We knew these weren't the "cool guys" on campus, but at the time it didn't matter. Their nerdiness was fun for us in that it made us feel cooler than we were. Filling up on free booze was our main objective and this place provided that with a nonthreatening atmosphere. The guys of Frat X never made passes at us or asked us to contribute money to new kegs. Light flirting and a feigned interest in their fraternity satisfied them enough that we kept coming back most weekend nights. Eventually Meredith and I would develop a sense of social rules to float around, but those first few months everywhere on campus with alcohol and new people was open to exploring.

As a college freshman you have an abundance of conditions working against you. You've recently been ripped from your comfortable childhood home where someone took care of all of your basic needs. You have to learn how to independently maintain a daily schedule, keep up with grades, not gain too much weight, make new friends, not get pregnant, become an expert in talking about sex, ensure that your parents think you're happy, and take care of yourself, all while figuring out your new identity as a quasi–sovereign adult. Despite all of this, college freshmen have one gift that like Cinderella's dream evening only lasts for a finite amount of time (and in this case someone is bound to come home missing a shoe and not remembering the guy she made out with as the clock struck midnight): the gift of social floating. In three years as upperclassmen in our sorority, Meredith and I will never party with the loser fraternities, off–brand sports team, or at the neighborhood stoner house. Social floating is the one thing that makes being a freshman special. You haven't established any roots and everyone assumes you're too naïve to know what you're doing, so it's the perfect time to do everything anywhere.

Those first months Meredith and I frequented anyone's house with an open door and full keg. We toured every sports house, bottom–rung fraternity, and even crashed random apartment parties because they were crowded and easy to blend into. Meredith and I had some of our most memorable and enjoyable nights of our freshman year hanging out with the gaggles of campus misfits. That year the two of us had very Wild West attitudes. We found that never having any money was thrilling and we loved figuring out ways (stealing) everything we wanted. Before leaving our dorm each night we made sure to bring multiple empty flasks and carry our biggest bags just in case we saw anything we couldn't live without. *Give me a signal if someone comes this way,* I would say to Meredith with my head in someone else's freezer stealing as much vodka as fast as I could. Meredith had an amazing ability to memorize number combinations and we used this power to steal unsuspecting boy's campus ID numbers to use to order pizza. *Let me see your ID picture,* she would say flirting with anyone who would hand over their card to her. *You look so cute,* she said while memorizing a 9 number combination in her brain then sending me a text with the code to free pizza. During a typical night out, we frequently dropped Ramen Noodles, Goldfish crackers, and entire cans of soup into our bags. Some mornings we would wake up with new DVDs, books, bottles of Advil, and,one time, a man's electric razor. Christmas came most mornings.

On one seemingly usual Thursday night at our favorite pregame house, Meredith and I stood around a keg trying to gag down a solo cup of half foam and half beer—we still hadn't perfected the art of pouring— we spent many nights swiping the oils off our noses and then twirling our oil slicked fingers around the cup to get rid of the excess foam–I don't recall if this trick worked, but I can't believe we didn't care how disgusting this was. Neither of us had acquired a taste for beer yet, and I let out a sigh complaining that I couldn't locate any liquor. Normally we managed to keep a water bottle of liquor on us at all times to avoid keg beer. At the beginning of each month my granny would send a card containing 20 dollars and a note to keep up the good work. This money was solely used for begging seniors to buy us a liter of flavored Burnett's vodka and allowing them to keep the change. Thinking back, it must have been the end of the month and we had run out our own stash and we patiently waited for my granny's letter to arrive.

After mere weeks of partying, the two of us had developed a nose for sniffing out who had what in a room. It took a 10–minute scan of the place to determine who had weed, pills, was DTF, and more importantly, who was hoarding the hard stuff. One of the frat brothers overheard us grumbling and mentioned he had a bottle of Burnett's vodka in the freezer. We smiled mischievously at one another and pounced on the poor boy. We couldn't believe someone was offering up his "good" vodka to us, so we both instinctively turned up the charm assuming we would need to flirt as a form of currency. I use the word "good" loosely. As a grown woman I recognize that Burnett's isn't top shelf, but it was a considerably large jump from our typical Aristocrat, which undoubtedly contains 45% rubbing alcohol.

Meredith began complimenting the guy and his friends as we both inched our way towards the kitchen. Just as our new favorite frat brother set up shot glasses, one of his roommates shouted, *Hey man! That vodka's mine! You can't just give it to those girls! I don't even know them.* As annoyed as I felt, I understood this guy's perspective, after all liquor doesn't grow on trees.

*Hi, I'm Sam,* I shouted across the kitchen. *We come here a lot and think your house is awesome. You guys are super cool.* I would have batted my eyelashes if they were capable of such a thing.

*Come on, man,* our favorite frat boy pleaded, *we'll just have one shot.*

The owner of the vodka walked over to us, shook our hands, and introduced himself. I remember this feeling too formal for the night and location. I rolled my eyes at Meredith and she sent a quick jab into my side rib and gave me a look that said, *Keep your eyes on the prize.* I hated having to work too hard for anything, and I was more of a loud mouth than a flirt, so I didn't have too many maneuvers in terms of getting guys to give me what I wanted. Luckily, guys typically looked at Meredith and gave her everything without question. She has a natural femininity to her that I have never embodied. She's one of those girls who looks sexy in sweatpants. The summer before we headed off to college she tried to teach me how to properly gel my hair to keep it curly and tame, and forced me to buy my first pair of designer jeans. Meredith always picked out my outfits when I couldn't make things coordinate, which was most nights.

*Ladies,* the vodka owner said in an obnoxious voice that sounded like he had watched *The Godfather* too many times, *I'll make a deal with you both. You girls kiss, just for a few seconds, and I'll give you as much of the vodka as you want.*

Meredith and I looked at each other, eyes wide, and simultaneously broke into hysterics. While the two of us were an affectionate duo, especially when buzzed, we had never kissed. I know from the outside this seemed like an obvious time for us to grab our things and leave; in fact, I think I've seen an episode of *Law And Order: SVU* that starts off in this exact scenario, but it's important to understand a few things: One being that this vodka is a hot commodity and something that could fuel an entire evening. Two, Meredith and I were living a real party monster stage in our lives and thrived on having crazy stories to tell our friends back home. Secretly, I had been patiently waiting for this day to arrive. I had been fantasizing about this exact college moment since I was freshman in high school. Part of me couldn't believe how fast my forced girl kissing fantasizing was coming to fruition. (Maybe *The Secret* was working!) After our laughing died down Frat *X* boy made us his offer one more time to show his seriousness. We looked at the vodka, and then at each with that *come on, we got this face* and told the guy he had a deal.

Before we could discuss a plan of action, the two guys corralled us onto a "stage" in the living room. I use the word *stage* loosely as it was merely pieces of plywood hammered together about three feet off the ground. (This is the same "stage" that just a few months later one of our friends will fall from while dancing, resulting in a torn meniscus. I can't remember how she explained that away to her parents, but I believe it required 6 weeks of physical therapy.) Within seconds, a group of frat guys surrounded us chanting *Kiss, kiss, kiss!* This exact moment might have also been in that same episode of *Law and Order: SVU*. Being surrounded by a bunch of drunk chanting guys was a horrifying experience, and as it turned out also the least sexy way to set up a kiss. The chanting felt like a threat, but I stayed calm by looking at Meredith. She laughed and twirled her hair around teasing the guys.

Her playfulness and ease calmed me down enough to catch my breath and not black out from fear.

For a drawn out 60 seconds, we stood there staring at each and laughing out in a panicked rhythm. The pressure set in. We knew we had about 30 seconds left to make this happen before the guys started booing, leaving us up there, and moving onto something new and shiny. At best, drunken frat guys have the attention span of newborn puppies. I felt panicked and heard my pulse beating out of wrist and throat. My fantasies about kissing a girl usually took place during a calm game of Spin the Bottle or Truth or Dare in a dim lit basement. In my fantasy I was already a little buzzed. The buzz was what gave me permission to indulge.

Now, I had never felt soberer. My armpits were sweating and by this time Meredith also looked stressed, so I had no calm left to hold onto. Then, without warning, she leaned in and kissed me. It happened all at once and in slow motion. I felt her tongue, and I couldn't believe how soft her lips felt against mine. I heard cheering in the distance, but before I could open my eyes it all ended. Meredith hopped off the stage and a group of guys ushered her into the kitchen. I stood on the stage frozen in place. My veins felt hot and my face flushed. Bolts of electricity ran through me. I'd kissed plenty of guys, but I had never experienced these sensations. I craved more of these feelings the second they wore off. This sober moment felt more intoxicating than any previous substance had made me feel. Obviously, I needed to immediately eliminate this feeling and make this overwhelming truth disappear.

Walking in a daze to the kitchen I felt terrified from

the knowledge that my new favored high did not come in an easy–to–swallow form. This new high that I sought would require human connection, vulnerability, and openness. The possibility of rejection would be high. I had plans to rush a sorority come spring, so continuing to toy with kissing girls felt out of the question.

Meredith stood in the kitchen, smiling, and handed me a full shot glass. *We've earned it,* she said full of accomplishment. I smiled and quickly knocked back the first drink. I then continued to pour in an attempt to forget and numb all the feelings that still lingered.

# Meeting Elliott Smith

While I'm not historically fan of Shawn Colvin or Steve Earle, I once found myself at a relatively intimate concert seeing them both. The show benefitted a school I worked at for children with autism, and I knew it would be insane to pass up the chance to hear "Sunny Came Home" live. I assumed I'd scroll through my phone until she played the one song I wanted to hear, but the moment Shawn stepped on stage my eyes only wanted to watch her. Shawn brought 90's Lilith Fair realness with her amazing quilted Technicolor Dream skirt, peasant top, and cowboy boots. At 61 her skin glowed immaculately and shone flawlessly even from the rear mezzanine of The Town Hall Theater. Her voice maintained a hypnotizing quality, reminiscent of honey and whiskey and she told fantastic personal stories between songs covering everything from relationships, politics, and her passion for song writing. Five minutes into her set, I accepted my new identity as a late in life Shawn Colvin fan. The woman was captivating.

Before introducing Steve Earle, she recounted an anecdote about a piece of shit ex–boyfriend from her past. The experience was tucked so far away that she couldn't recall exact details of his offenses, but she did retain that the one lasting thing he gave her was Steve Earle's album *Guitar Town*. She pinpointed the place she stood in his home when she heard Steve Earle's voice for the first time. Shawn revealed that *Guitar Town* would go on to be one of the most influential albums in her personal life and that the album aided in defining and shaping her personal musical writing style.

Amy Schumer discloses a similar story about hearing the magical voice of Otis Redding for the first time while having a less than pleasant hookup with a guy she didn't care much about. I assume many of us have comparable tales. These narratives are exact and transformative for both women and speak to the human condition of how we will desperately seek out something meaningful and beautiful even in the most unsatisfying moments, or maybe we seek even harder in these particular uncomfortable encounters. We are spurred to find silver linings and discover even the slightest lesson learned from inopportune moments. Accomplishing this allows us to believe our suffering, no matter how small, was worth experiencing. I've wondered if the music is elevated to something higher during these times of need like a siren distraction call. Once, in a similar moment of desperation, I met Elliott Smith in the backseat of a car.

The first semester of my freshman year, I walked down into the basement of a Hockey Team party. I had walked down those stairs numerous times but that evening my eyes immediately noticed one guy. He wasn't particularly handsome or involved in what appeared to be a riveting conversation. I didn't recognize him at all, but it wasn't his newness that drew my eyes to him in an instant – it was his balls. His testicles hung casually out of the front of his pants. His light scrotum against his army green hue pants made quite the contrast. I watched as he carried himself in a nonchalant manner, refilling his beer from the keg and laughing with a friend. I made a beeline for him. As someone who frequently engaged in social experiments of my own I had to meet this guy. Hi, I said. *Are you new to the team? I've never seen you before. Also, it appears your balls have spilled out of your pants.*

*Hi,* he said clinking his Solo cup against mine. *I'm actually just visiting a friend this weekend. I go to Virginia Tech.* I continued sipping my beer, staring at his balls, and not speaking. *Also, yes my balls are out. They're a little claustrophobic,* he said in the same tone one would use when talking about a poorly behaved child. I laughed and that was it; we didn't discuss his low hanging fruit any further.

It turned out he was an English major, which I swooned over. Seeing as I spent most of my times with sports teams and frat guys, I had mostly only met business and communication majors up to that point, and they spent most of their time bragging about how fast they could shotgun a beer. I immediately began probing this mysterious nerd about his favorite authors and books. It became obvious that this was probably my first actual conversation I'd had at a party with a guy. Usually, it was just 10 minutes of awkward chit chat about freshman life before I had my tongue down some guy's throat in a bathroom, bedroom, rooftop, on a park bench, against the side of a house, or occasionally in the corner of a party, but that was less preferred as it felt tacky. Balls Out sounded intelligent and passionate. He told me that he eventually wanted to be a college professor. Obviously, I swooned again. I brought up Virginia Woolf hoping he'd have something to say. Spoiler: harboring a lifelong obsession with Virginia Woolf is a good indicator that you're most likely a likely lesbian, but no one had told me that yet, so I rambled on about her works and personal life while trying to explain to him where I found parallels between the two. He followed my meandering and mentioned that he read *Mrs. Dalloway* a few semesters ago and *really liked it*. Continuing he suggested I read *A Room of One's Own,* as if I hadn't already. Although he didn't add an original theory and seemed to be merely dropping book titles, I was practically drooling as the words left his mouth. My excitement level reached a new apex; a straight man was telling me he loved to read and write, could list multiple books, and had collegiate professional aspirations. *This guy must be special,* I thought. Maybe I was finally meeting someone I could tolerate longer than a one–night stand.

We spent the next hour drinking and finding commonalities in our taste in music and movies. I made sure to frequently touch his arm throughout our conversation and exaggerated my laugh when he said anything remotely funny as a way to make sure he knew I was flirting. *Do you want to get out of here?* he asked when it looked like the party was migrating next door. It was the first time someone had used that line on me (is this even considered a line?) and I didn't care. I couldn't wait to get my mouth on his as we walked out of the house. We walked down the street holding hands and it felt like something you only did with someone you really liked. This guy must be different.

A short stroll later, we were making out in his car parked in the back of a church. My dorm was just a 10–minute walk away, so I'm not sure how we settled on this being the best make out spot. My expectations were highly unattainable from the start. I wanted to feel as passionate about kissing him as I did talking to him. I needed the intellectual butterflies to turn into erotic ones. I ran my hands through his hair and kissed his neck, as those were actions I saw women doing in movies and on TV when they really liked a guy. This was my best attempt in showing him, and myself, how into all of this I was. A brief five minutes into the kissing, I disappointingly realized I didn't feel any butterflies, intellectual, erotic, or otherwise. This empty feeling felt furiously typical and I had become accustomed to this general hurried loss of passion with guys. Most nights, my disappointment allowed me to continue on with the hook up, as I would decide that a lackluster orgasm might as well substitute my sudden sense of hollowness.

While the kissing progressed, I silently debated in my head whether or not I should fuck The Professor in the backseat of his car. As I carefully weighed my options he tried to gracefully maneuver my hand into his already unzipped pants. He obviously didn't need to create a mental checklist to decide where he wanted things to go. That night the emptiness within myself felt deeper than usual. I hated that the spark

I felt earlier with him dissipated. As I attempted to keep my hand on the outside his pants I wished I had left this at a good conversation and had gone to 7–11 with Meredith for late night taquitos and Cherry Coke Big Gulps. It was too late. My obsession with wanting to force a meaningful connection from mere shared interests led me into the backseat of this cramped four door that I was just noticing smelled like a gym bag. All at once I felt too sober for the experience. While I successfully kept my keep my hands away from his hard on, I noticed the music filling up the car. It was a voice that I had never heard before, and it matched my forlorn void precisely.

*Who is this singing?* I asked while trying to politely push my way up from a lying position.

*Elliott Smith,* The Professor said quickly and then began to kiss down my neck while unhooking my bra. Giving over, I laid back down and let The Professor continue to kiss me. I opened my eyes to look at the upside church outside. I rubbed the fogged window to see more clearly; a light from the inside caused the stain glass to glow like a nightlight. I let a sigh of disappointment, but this sound registered to the professor as sign of pleasure and he began kissing my collarbone and neck with even more gusto.

*It's beautiful. And deeply depressing,* I said continuing to stare outside.

*He killed himself over an ex–girlfriend,* I think, he said between breaths. My brain wanted to hear more songs by Elliot Smith – and to be alone. At this point The Professor tried to guide my hand again towards his exposed self. I rerouted his hand to my chest in an attempt to be playful but mostly as an act of avoidance; I admired his polite persistence.

After another five minutes of kissing and avoiding his dick passed, I realized I didn't feel like pretending any longer or fucking in the back seat of this car. I assertively sat up. *I need to go,* I said as I exited the car with an unhooked bra. Not having the energy to re–hook it I pulled my bra completely off and stuffed it into my bag. My deflated sense of self didn't allow me to even enjoy the sensation of walking around with free breasts. I sent out a text to everyone I knew on campus trying to avoid going back to the dorm. The experience left me craving a few more drinks before bed; I needed the fill the vacancy with something. No one responded. It was that point in the night when people were passed out, hooking up, or eating something happily in their pajamas.

When I arrived back to the dorm Meredith was entertaining a catch of her own, and sweetly asked me to hang out in the bathroom. I quickly grabbed my laptop, headphones, and a pillow before shutting myself into the communal space. I pulled Elliott Smith up on YouTube and listened to everything I could find while reading about this tragic and short–lived life. Elliott was the gem pulled from my shit pile of a night that I needed. While I may not have made an actual human connection, I did receive an artist who connected me to the night and my feelings. *Art is forever and people are merely seasons,* I thought consoling myself. Hitting *play* on my newly crafted playlist, I let the sadness fill me and closed my eyes, allowing myself to nod off on the bathroom floor.

# I Forgot His Name;
# It Was Gross

Modern psychology theory on trauma states people who have experienced trauma may subconsciously go on to find ways to recreate it even years after the event has occurred. This hypothesis theorizes the subconscious wants to perfect the trauma, or gain mastery over the experience, as it was once something completely out of the person's control. Victims of trauma often find themselves in similar situations attempting to control key specific aspects and have an opportunity to re–manage their feelings. Some find themselves consistently dating abusive partners and others may enter dangerous situations knowing the high risks. (ie: Many soldiers returning form war suffering from PTSD return and secure physically high risk jobs.)

While often subconscious, I found myself retraumatizing myself in a variety of patterns and poor decisions making. For me, the idea of sex was an opportunity to regain the agency over my body and sexuality that I had lost as a child. At times, the sense of control appeared genuine and left me feeling powerful. During these highs, it was as if I was finally in charge of the sexual happenings to my body. The sense of power usually came down swiftly, however, as I hiked home in the middle of the night from some stranger's apartment, or found myself shoving a guy out of my front door with a litany of excuses for him not being able to stay the night. Following most encounters, my body rang with anxiety and a heavy weight settled into my chest.

In my plan to rediscover my sexual footing I mainly ended up triggering my body and no matter how many flares it sent up telling me to stop, I wouldn't listen. I'm lucky; the majority of my sexual experiences left me unscathed. Most guys just wanted to have fun and followed all my verbal commands; most importantly of which *it's time for you to leave*. A few incidents feel gray and the control I desperately craved didn't always manifest. Looking back, trying to examine the situations objectively, I've never been able to ascertain a pattern of why some sexual situations yielded the results I desired and some fell short. The right experience could leave me feeling boisterous and self–assured, but more often than I not, I was left saturated in shame and lacking.

As the wise Carrie Bradshaw once asked: "Are we behaving as a victims of trauma or are we just sluts?"

## The Astronaut

I was a party freshman year in a place I wouldn't dare step foot in just one year later when I met The Astronaut. Like The Professor, this guy alleged to be from out of town visiting a friend at our school. Huddled around a game of beer pong, he told me he was from Florida and was training to be an astronaut.

While this sounds like one of the lamest, most obvious lies to ever be uttered by a guy, it wasn't until about five years later that I realized his story probably wasn't true. In his defense, saying you're training to be a literal astronaut is a creative and charming pick–up line, like saying you're a volunteer firefighter times 1000. A career that involves both brains and tremendous courage – such a smart scam! At the time, I truly believed him and was once again blinded by the idea that he was brilliant. Also at the time, I was brilliantly wasted and constantly on the search for someone who seemed different and special. Of course, I went back with him to his friend's dorm (although maybe it was actually his own dorm?! Am I finally putting together all the pieces?), and I immediately had sex with him. How could I have passed up the opportunity to sleep with a real live astronaut in training?

Typical to my experience, I couldn't make it through more than half of the sexual encounter before checking out. His timid hands and rapid movements pushed him off the pedestal of my creation and, as usual, I just wasn't that turned on. In the span of 20 minutes he went from genius–almost–astronaut to just another boy I would soon feel ashamed of fucking. After he finished, he got up to go to the bathroom to do whatever it is guys do after they have sex, I'm unsure. (Do they also need to pee right after in order to not get a UTI too? Or are they in there high fiving themselves for putting their dick in a human woman?) *I'll be back for round two, just give me a minute.* He said with too much bravado for someone who came in under three minutes. I didn't even pretend to reach orgasm, so his assured voice surprised my ears. Having no idea how long I had until he returned, I sprung up, hurried into my pants, and slipped on my shoes. Still topless, I threw off the sheets and ducked under the bed looking for the rest of my clothes.

As I sifted through the mess of dirty socks, crumbled papers, and pulverized cigarettes, I knew I likely only had mere seconds before he returned, so I needed to make a quick decision about what to do with my missing bra and shirt. Unable to form a decent plan under my self–imposed pressure, I grabbed his shirt from the floor and pulled it over my head as I ran out the dorm room and flew down the closest staircase I could find. I continued running once I exited the building and kept up a pace like I was being chased by a masked killer in a trashy horror/porno film until I reach the next dorm feeling all the while like he might be paces behind me, which of course he wasn't. This is as close as I will every come to ghosting someone. Looking back, I am unsure why I didn't simply shout, *I'm out of here. Thanks for the weak lay. Good luck on Mars.* Once a shrink told me that I appeared to create and seek out chaos, which is a fairly typical pattern for people live in a world of constant fight or flight, not knowing how to function in a steady place.

Slowing down I walked the rest of the home mourning my bra and shirt knowing I'd never see them again. My skin lit up and my thighs began to itch – all sensations egging me to self–harm.

*How was it?* Meredith asked. *You're back earlier than I expected.*

*He was clumsy…such a boy,* I said as I turned on the

shower hoping the scalding water would tamper the sudden uncomfortable squirminess in my skin.

Internally, I was starting to feel unsure about these casual sexual encounters. A part of me loved how I felt in control, wanted, and sophisticated for my seemingly unattached emotions, but I hated the speed in which these feeling faded. For the moment, it was convenient to blame a guy's lack of experience and not look inwards.

## The Marine

By the time I met him my stomach held at least four shots of vodka and likely two beers. I was no longer an ingénue freshman, but a well–oiled self–destruction machine in my third year. No longer did I attempt to seek out guys for attempts at making emotional connections or to try to ignite a feeling of passion. I knew I was using them as a means to hurt, control, and occasionally feel good about myself. About 50 of us crammed into a frat basement, which provided no relief from the summer heat that felt excessively stifling and damp even by Virginia standards. He was enormous in a way that didn't typically interest me with thick muscles pressing through a white t–shirt and standing a foot and some inches taller than me. His body and demeanor rattled my insides with uncertainty though I knowingly targeted him. I walked towards with him no intent other than amplifying my initial feelings of discomfort. He spoke with an accent, or slur, that I couldn't place and said he had been kicked out of the Marines. The ex–Marine didn't attend our school but lived in our rural town and partied like a seasoned coed. My brain holds no formative recollection of our conversation.

As the evening continued, I fueled myself with more drinks pushing myself towards him. At the time, fear felt more like an emotion worth chasing than a warning sign of physical or mental danger ahead. Regard for my well–being was essentially nonexistent, and I craved various forms of self–inflicted violence. Once acceptably intoxicated, I led him back to my apartment where we engaged in mundane sex. When we met I felt certain about his propensity towards violence and tried without avail to nudge him on to be rougher with me. Afterwards I begrudgingly started to get dressed as he sat on the edge of my bed already tying his shoes. *At least he didn't want to stay,* I thought. We began exchanging the type of pleasantries that one gives after such a swift interaction when I said, *I've actually had better sex with women.*

This sentence was a lie, although a hopeful one. The words bruised what I assume was his fragile idea of masculinity and before the last word left my tongue he slammed me against the wall and held me in place with one hand – middle finger to bottom of palm appeared to extend the length of chest. My bones sank inward from the weight of his heavy hand. I knew I had sensed an ominous presence in him. A moment later my body slammed back onto my bed as he hovered above me spouting vulgarities. I attempted to stand up and breeze past him, but he backed up blocking the door. While he continued to rant I sent a *S–O–S* text to my friend who lived next door. By the grace of coming home last and being mostly blacked out, the front door was never locked, and my friend stormed in causing a racket and easily extricated him.

Although I located the disorder that I sought, I didn't feel fuller after the experience. The violence I had orchestrated left my insides lacking anything substantial and I realized I might be number than when the night began. My life had become a game of throwing emotionally charged darts at myself hoping anything would stick. Back at my friend's house, the first memory I have is sitting on her kitchen floor surrounded by bubbly drunken sorority girls eating pizza. The event wasn't discussed much further and I shoved it down as deep as I could, although this exercise was getting more difficult to accomplish as events were rapidly piling up.

## Mr. Pussy

Mr. P was a little different than my random one–time run–ins. I met him at a summer orientation and he lived two doors down from Meredith and me. We were all buddies the first months of school during the time when you cling to everyone around you for social safety. His nickname to most people was Skulls. This was given to him by a bunch of jocks at the lacrosse house where we all used to hang out. Our college was small, rural, conservative, and therefore moderately preppy. Skulls looked out of place. His outfits consisted of combat boots and various punk rock tee shirts. None of these items were worn with irony. He was also short; we met eye to eye at my meager 5 foot 3 inch stature. I liked talking to him.

Mr. P wasn't like any of the guys I knew from

school. He wanted to talk about music and politics. The guys we hung around with always gave him a hard time. Skulls would have been better suited at a hippie art college in the mountains or somewhere more urban. The red line that we lived on in Virginia wasn't a great fit for anyone outside of the considered norm, i.e., jocks, sorority girls, fraternity boys, Christians, heterosexuals, and white people. I barely slid by being obviously white, femme, and in a sorority. Skulls didn't care that the jocks ragged on him; he even thought his nickname was a sort of stamp of approval. He didn't want to be liked by them anyways which I was deeply impressed by.

One night when we were walking home from a party, we stood at a corner waiting to cross a street, and he kissed me seemingly out of nowhere. I didn't know if I had feeling for him but the kiss felt sweet and sincere. He invited me to his dorm room to listen to the Sex Pistols and introduce me to English punk. I assumed listening to music was code for hooking up. I quickly realized that for what Skulls lacked in height and social coolness, he made up for in his giving nature. After this evening I wouldn't have cared if he was 3'6," I would happily *come over and listen to punk*, whenever Mr. P wanted me there.

At first things were great. I would arrive to his dorm late at night, hardly reciprocate, never have sex, and then promptly leave. It was my perfect scenario. Some nights before or after the hooking up, we would smoke a blunt and he would give me mini lessons from his musical world. One night I told him my life long secret of listening to small doses of punk. *I actually love Slipknot...and Korn,* I said to him. *In high school I fantasized about moving to Portland, giving myself a hideous haircut, and becoming a riot grrl groupie.*

*Why did it take you so long to tell me? I knew I could see something different in you,* he said as if secretly listening to Bikini Kill was something that you could see on a person. I swore him to secrecy. While no longer resided in my preppy high school and knew no one would care if they found out, it was a secret I liked keeping to myself. Not surprisingly, problems quickly arose between us. Mr. P wanted to talk about his feelings, often. He liked to tell me how he thought I was so different than other girls he had met, and he would say how well he would treat me if we could really be together as a couple. He didn't understand why I didn't want to spend the night at his place or even cuddle. Mr. P would get frustrated when I didn't want to meet him for coffee, or come over to actually watch a movie. He wanted more than just a hook–up. And he was right; I wasn't like most girls he knew. Most girls would be thrilled to have a sweet, giving guy want to not only hook up but also hang out and get to know them. I'm sure he would have been an excellent boyfriend.

Within a few weeks he stopped returning my texts and didn't want me to come over anymore. I felt sad that I couldn't give him more of myself, and furious for not fully understanding why. As much as I liked the idea of him, I knew he would see through me – making my usual pretending impossible. Months passed before we spoke again, although we did occasionally smirk at another in the hall. After an initial cooldown, we continued to meet up and fell back into physically entangling ourselves every few months for the next three years. Each time he would profess to me that I should give him a chance and tell me we could be good together. And every time I would throw him his shirt at him and show him the door.

We had sex once, and it was the last time I saw him.

The fall of our senior year I was walking home from a party and found him smoking on a lawn alone with raucous house full of people behind him. It was late and the weather was just starting to turn. The air was almost chilly and the smell of fall leaves filled me with newness. It had been six months since we last saw one another. We exchanged knowing smiles and without asking, he walked me home without saying more than a handful of words. Sex ensued and it was a disaster. He moved too fast, acted too eager, and there was no giving. By this point, he knew the procedure and didn't propose sleeping over. I felt gross and couldn't get him out of the apartment fast enough. Before he finished locating his wallet and keys, I collected my bed sheets, and dumped them into the wash, starting a load, not caring about the noise or hour of night. I couldn't tolerate having the smell of him or the experience of what had happened on my skin for another second. My whole body crawled with agitation and thoughts of cutting my skin open raced through my head.

After locking the door behind him I tore off my remaining clothes and climbed into the shower where I began scrubbing myself as hard as I could in attempt to remove any microscopic remaining molecules of his off of me. The water pressure wasn't hard enough and despite my skin glowing red, I couldn't get the water hot enough to feel like it was killing off the lingering particles. Having sex with him triggered a spot inside me that I had worked tirelessly to keep away from. Living in this state of limbo was proving more difficult each day.

It was also becoming increasingly arduous to keep her out of my head.

# Illuminate

**M**eredith and I giggled our way into the bathroom pushing past a sea of drunk coeds at a lacrosse house party. *Me first*, she said pulling her jeans down and hovering above the toilet as not to let her skin come in contact with the typically filthy seat. I playfully shoved her slightly off balance and then settled on the edge of the bathtub facing directly towards her. In less than 10 seconds, I gulped down the majority of my keg beer and offered her the remaining sips. Meredith finished off the drink and tossed the red plastic cup into the tub behind me as if she shooting a winning basket.

*Do you think you'll go home with Brian?* I asked as she wiped herself, flushed, and stood up pulling her jeans and underwear back into position with one expert swoop. Instinctively, we switched places.

*Maybe, depending how drunk he gets,* she said.

*Yeah, you don't need any more whiskey dick in your life,* I said sending us into a collective fit of giggles as I pulled down my pants to sit. Meredith's laugh abruptly stops, but I continued giggling a few beats behind the situation. I couldn't pull her gaze towards mine and noticed she was staring at my leg. In too late of an attempt I covered the rusty scabs that zig zag across my thigh to break her stare.

*You have to go get help for this,* Meredith said standing above me yelling from what looked like fear. Her voice cracked and broke into a cry I can hardly comprehend. *I don't understand this. Please talk to me. I don't get it and you're scaring me. I don't want to call your parents, but I don't know what to do.* Meredith sat back down on the edge of tub and stared blankly at me waiting for a response.

I finished buttoning up my jeans defensively and stood leaning against the sink staring at the floor, but not trying to completely escape the situation. Meredith and I had been best friends since high school, and she knew I had a history of cutting, but we had never fully discussed it other than me telling her things were in control and her telling me I could talk to her if I ever wanted. Part of me liked that she knew as it took the edge off of the overwhelming isolation.

Historically, cutting was a private behavior that I engaged and found solace in for numerous reasons. I loved the ritual, the ultimate sense of control, and the physical sensations akin to a high. Mostly though, I needed it to quiet down my skin, which was an often uncomfortable place to live in and cutting was the only way I knew how to shut it up and make it stop screaming at me. No one would ever expect you to hold in a sneeze or not tend to a bug bite, so while cutting was entrenched in shame, it also seemed reasonable. Even the after effects were enjoyable; feeling the way my wound burned through a pair of jeans when the scar rubbed against it as I walked the halls between classes sustained some secret pain inside of me. I loved staring at the scar knowing that their concreteness made feeling awful make more sense. Cutting is powerful. It allows you to play all the parts of a traumatic situation in one moment. You get to fill the role of victim, perpetrator, and helper. No one leaves her skin open and bleeding, so you literally have the opportunity to wipe the wound clean and bandage yourself up, physically and emotionally. For control seekers like myself, it's the ultimate experience. Cutting provided a sense of comfort and from an early age, I found all of it a complicated and addictive process.

When college began, my cutting tremendously escalated, most likely because I had no one to report to or ballet tights to expose myself in. I was free to hide my skin as needed. While occurring at higher rates, I still felt in control of the situation and didn't see it as a big deal. *I just have a different way of managing my emotions,* I had always told myself. That night in the bathroom was the first time I told Meredith about my childhood, the older boy, being sexually assaulted, and how I wasn't sure it was related but all of it felt connected in a way I couldn't explain. *Where is he? I'll kill him,* Meredith said through tears. While the notion sounded ridiculous and juvenile, I had never felt more loved or seen than in that moment. I promised Meredith I would call campus counseling in the morning.

Once the sober light of day hit, I dreaded making the call to set up an appointment knowing I held no honest intention of giving up my behaviors, but I didn't want Meredith to carry the weight of my choices so I obliged her request to seek help. Besides, the service didn't cost anything and I thought I might end up meeting a young male graduate student to seduce, thus achieving my lifelong fantasy of attaining the most unattainable. Men under 25 have hardly developed their frontal lobes and I realized this process might prove too easy.

After completing what felt like an over–revealing phone intake, the counseling center matched me up with young graduate student named Ann, and I immediately lost interest in my seduction fantasy knowing that women are too serious and I'd never entice her into anything beyond her professional boundaries. *Hi, thanks for coming in, I'm glad to see you,* Ann said shaking my hand and using her other hand as a Vanna White arm to introduce me to her shitty, barren graduate student office space. She completed her own intake similar to the one I did over the phone with the main office. I was already annoyed at the repetitiveness of the process.

*I told them this already,* I kept saying while she nodded and took notes. I filled out a rating scale that seemed familiar; *maybe Dr. Shayne used something like it,* I thought to myself. Nothing here appeared new, which felt calming and like I was one step ahead already.

*Our sessions will be recorded,* Ann said, *and I need you to sign this form saying you're okay with this. I'll review our weekly sessions with my supervisor for support and get guidance to better help you,* she said. Although I knew Ann was a graduate student when I made the appointment, hearing her say that a supervisor would help her to help me made me feel superior, and I immediately looked down on her. Likely, this was a way in which for me to evade focus from myself and keep my attention on her. *Well I won't need any supervision or guidance to continue fucking myself up,* I said to which she didn't laugh, but I maintain to this day that is a solid therapy joke (feel free to try out if the situation arises!). I left the first session consenting to everything and signing each line nodding and smiling.

*I look forward to working with you,* she said on my way out.

*You too,* I said, walking down the hall listening to the collective *swooshing* sounds of the white noise machines placed neatly outside identical doors.

---

*Why do you think you told me you did cocaine this weekend?* Ann asked during our third or fourth session.

*You asked what I did over the weekend,* I said back with confusion.

*Do you think you want to tell me about any issues with drugs you might have?* She continued.

*Are you implying I have a problem with drugs? That sounds a little leading,* I said looking at her firmly. I loved nothing more than randomly hurling therapy words at her in an attempt to make her feel like she had said the wrong thing. During our 50 minutes, I tossed my feelings of discomfort back to her like a game of Hot Potato. Throughout our sessions, I have watched Ann go from ingénue therapist to self–conscious and fatigued. We had developed a dynamic in which I went out of my way to make her feel inadequate and uncomfortable while she tried to play hard with me with no authority and a shaky voice that didn't fool either one of us.

*I want to know what it feel likes to have my heart broken* I said in a rare moment of truthfulness. Recently, I'd watched Meredith fall in love only to have her heart stomped on and I'd never seen so much symbiotic pain between two people. It looked desperate and consuming in a way I'd never experienced with another person and I wanted in.

*Do you think it's possible you might not be attracted to guys?* she asked following up my statement catching me completely off guard (although it shouldn't have as in weeks prior I had talked about my obsession with a handful of girls and had confided in my general loathing and lack of honest sexual interest with the guys I slept with).

*Can you even ask me that? I can't believe you said that.* I said staring at her long enough to cause her skin to change from white to pink to red as my eyes buried into her. Staring, I waited for her response, not feeling the need to speak again or fill the room with noise. If she could sit in silence, so could I.

*It wouldn't be a problem if you didn't like them,* she said attempting to muster back her authority.

*Obviously. I know gay people, I have gay people in my family, but that doesn't mean you can call me gay.* I said trying to make her feel awful but mostly terrified that she saw me. I hated how obvious of a dyke I was.

After two more weeks we both knew our relationship wasn't going anywhere, and she recommended a resource outside of campus called the Women's Resource Center. As much as I resisted the idea of changing my behavior, I did have to admit I liked having someone's full attention and having my feelings be taken seriously by a professional, so I called and set up an appointment.

On a blustery but sunny winter day, I circled the street looking for the WRC. The wind stung my eyes and I passed the place twice before I realized which building it was. I was searching for a professional clinical–looking setting, but found the operation to be run out of a shabby house looking like it could belong to a local townie. After checking in I was asked to fill out more paperwork. As I checked boxes and circled symptoms, I couldn't understand why my school wouldn't just fax over the essay of work I had filled out for them already. *Maybe this was an exercise in accepting that I needed help,* I thought.

Dread hung over me, and my foot shook with anxiety, thinking about having to meet someone new. My record of feeling connected to therapists was 0 for 2, so I wasn't filled with optimism. A moment later, an older woman, post 50, rounded the corner and greeted me with the twang accent of someone who had been raised in a rural southern town. Her light energy evoked an involuntary smile and allowed my leg to momentarily quiet down. *You must be Samantha, or do you go by Sam? You look like a Sam to me. I'm Betty and I'm so happy you came in.*

*All my friends call me Sam,* I said staring at her crow's feet proving years of living. Immediately I wanted to trust her, likely due to a combination of her syrupy voice and natural confidence. Right away it felt like she had everything under control. A sensation to crawl up into her lap and be rocked flooded me. Betty was like an older, less glamorous, backwoods version of Stevie

Nicks. She wore long flowing skirts and loose peasant tops. Her office resembled a cross between the sale section at Michaels Craft Store and a summer solstice Wicca ritual ceremony. Two large windows flooded her office with bright natural sunlight, even in the middle of January. Crystals, dream catchers, rain sticks, and stacks of empty journals scattered throughout the room. She insisted I pick a journal and began writing in it the first day we met. Betty left stress balls and various objects to manipulate for fidgety hands within arm's reach. I preferred the classic squeeze guy whose eyes popped out.

My instinct to manipulate and control uncomfortable situations didn't flare up, which allowed me to honestly talk and feel heard. It never felt like she had a hidden agenda or passed judgment on me. Her voice and face remained calm and collected no matter what I spoke about. We made collages for past traumatic events that I couldn't yet find the words for. Although I often protested declaring everything as "stupid," I followed through with her suggestions to write a letter to my younger self, keep a journal, and attempt to learn what it meant to ground yourself. *That was stupid*, I said to her smiling when I finished reading the letter I wrote out loud. I didn't need to tell her that the exercise did in fact provide some comfort as she understood me by that point and winked knowingly.

Week after week I showed up, sat down, and talked. I opened up and showed her my ugliest wounds. Every session felt like lemon juice being poured into fresh paper cuts. I hated going, but I noticed my brain clearing up and my skin feeling calmer. My body yelled at me less and it didn't feel tight as often. Seeing Betty allowed me to realize that being in that bedroom, repeatedly, as a girl wasn't my fault. I was 19 and the revelation meant everything. Maybe I wasn't a slut or bad or gross or an inherent fuck–up, but I was just understandably sad and confused. Betty helped me differentiate my own voice from my trauma, which had spent a lifetime telling me I would never be good enough and I was broken on the inside. While this didn't make the negative thoughts completely disappear, I did begin to uncover the sound of my true self. I don't know why I stopped seeing Betty after only six months. The work probably became too challenging and I had no interest in wholly giving up my cycle of vices (sex, drinking/drugs, and self–injury). Seeing her, however, did aid me in toning down my habits to a more manageable level, and cracked myself open enough for a little light to start seeping in.

# Save Me

*Be aware it's just your mind. And you can stop it anytime. Save me.*

—Jem

I repeated these lyrics to myself steadily throughout the summer before my senior year of college. While I knew Jem had written this song with a facetious intent, I needed to believe her. *Stop thinking about her, I would tell myself. Stop fantasizing about touching her skin, smelling her neck, and running your lips over hers. Stop being such a dyke,* I said in my head, berating myself. I wanted to annihilate all delusional thoughts about her from my psyche. I didn't want to love her. All summer I tried desperately to make myself feel any romantic spark for a guy. I needed to know I could have feelings for someone other than her, and it would be helpful if I could have them for a guy. At a minimum, meaning at a minimum I had other options; I wasn't ready to commit to being a full–blown, lifelong lesbian. I could manage the idea of being bisexual, but only in an easy, sexy way, not in a head–over–heels, I–only–want–

to–love–you–for–the–rest–of–my–life kind of way. No back–up plan for managing my feelings existed. Believing in the achievability of Plan A was my only viable option. My brain rattled with worry that if I couldn't attain this goal I would likely go insane.

*We're too entangled,* I texted her one afternoon while washing dishes at the cafe I worked it during the summer. I happily took orders to wash dishes, as it was the only area in the cafe no one would yell at you for texting, and seeing as we spent most hours of the day texting I needed this freedom. *There's no way this will end well,* I continued to text. *You make me happier than anyone. How will the boys compete? You might have to just marry me. We've all seen* Will and Grace*; we know these types of relationships never end well.* I had attempted to send a text denoting that we could both benefit from some emotional space, but I couldn't form the right sentence and I knew it came across as a desperate plea to love me. We had sent bold flirtatious texts to each other in the past, but this one felt particularly obvious and my heart raced waiting for a response. In order to grow feelings for a guy, I assumed I needed to create emotional space from her, but I also secretly hoped that idea would send her into a tailspin and force her to come to terms with her feelings for me.

*Am I Will or Grace* she responded in an instant. Her text rambled and continued *We'll live next door to each other and have sleepovers when our husbands are out of town, don't worry so much,* she replied. She actively ignored the anguish and seriousness of my text. The seeming immaturity of her response infuriated me and deepened my feelings of isolation. At times, it was difficult gauging her true sentiments. In some moments, like this, she would act oblivious to the convoluted "friendship" we created. While other times she seemed more aware and I would get a text at night saying, *I miss you. Wish you were in here with me. I sleep better with you.* Or my favorite: *I'm taking you on a date this weekend. Can't wait to see you.* I reread both of those texts hundreds of times over making sure I wasn't hallucinating the words I craved to see. *Taking you on a date. I sleep better with you. Date. Sleep. You. With me. Date. Better with you.* Each word stuck to my insides and filled with me possibility.

*Insecurities keep growing, Wasted energies are flowing, Anger, pain and sadness beckon, Panic sets in in a second, Be aware it's just your mind you can stop it anytime*

She sounded calm when I told her about Ryan. I met him in downtown Richmond at my friend's sister's party over the weekend and I decided I liked him because he was five years older than the rest of us. It was exciting hearing him talk about life, post college. Telling Alissa that Ryan and I were going out that weekend on a date she listened attentively and I strained listening for signs of discomfort on her end, but found none. *You should give him a chance,* she said after I finished a ramble in which I attempted to convince the two of us that I actually wanted to partake in this date. *He sounds nice,* she said. As if "nice" is a hot commodity or a personal characteristic to be valued. My jaw tightened as we spoke and I ached for her to tell me not to go. I was already having difficulty keeping up with this facade of "girl likes boy" and I hadn't even been on the date yet. I felt myself unraveling. I couldn't decipher reality from my imagination. Maybe I didn't understand the difference between regular friendship and romantic love. Or worse maybe, I had turned into caricature of a dyke who falls for her best friend. *Have fun tonight and let me know how it goes. Text me when you get home. And try to be nice.* she said before we hung up.

Ryan picked me up right on time and came inside to meet my parents. His manners, full–time job, and aroma of something other than Axe Body Spray impressed them. Usually, I brought around potheads and frat guy types who waited in their car for me to come out without even a honk or wave in my parent's directions. The bar wasn't hard to clear. Ryan took me to his apartment before dinner. When I entered his surprisingly spacious and tidy place, a slobbery dog immediately accosted me, though Ryan said that meant she liked me. He went on to add that his dog always assists him in picking out his new girlfriends without a hint of sarcasm in his voice. I smiled petting the dog trying to look amused. *Can I have a drink?* I asked as I walked through his house perusing through all his belongings without asking. *Can I use your bathroom?* I asked already headed in that direction. Rifling through his medicine cabinet I examined each piece like an archeologist. Contents included Tylenol, Band Aids, Condoms, Blue Polo Cologne, razor, and multiple hair gels. No sense to steal anything overwhelmed me with disappointment. As I begin raking through his closet I finished my second beer. His closet was comprised of every imaginable color Polo shirt and pastels and patterns of khaki type pants imaginable. Ryan represented the perfectly quaffed Southern gentleman. I counted three "different" pairs of loafers and ridiculed him for this. He interpreted my mocking as flirting. Laughing he told me my curiousness about his possessions was cute. Being cute seemed important. *I'm just nosy* I said. Historically, guys have mistaken my light harassment as flirting, and I wonder if this is a defense mechanism or do men think it's impossible that a woman would slightly insult them on a first date?

We went to dinner at a Vietnamese restaurant where he excitedly ordered for me. He had plans of going to Southeast Asia in the spring, and wanted to know where I had traveled. *The Caribbean and Mexico*, I replied. *I don't know if that counts,* I said sucking a shrimp out of my translucent spring roll. I drained three more beers throughout dinner. Towards the end of the meal my buzz fully set, allowing me to relax and decide maybe I liked that he was smart and had a cute dog. It seemed admirable that he already owned his own apartment. Though I hated his pants, littered with crabs, whales, or some other nautical creature that did not belong on a grown man. My sudden sense of positivity made me assume I could overlook this transgression. He made me laugh, twice. The drinks encouraged me to give him a try. He was nice after all.

As we drove up to my house I asked him to pull his car in front of the lawn, avoiding the driveway. Ryan killed the engine and said he had a nice night and wondered aloud if he could see me again while keeping his eyes straight ahead. I unbuckled my seat belt and leaned over to kiss him. He kissed me back, and I crawled into the backseat of his Jeep pulling him with me. I continued to kiss him, not because I was filled with an overwhelming desire, but because my brain rang like an alarm with an overwhelming panic knowing I didn't want him despite him being nice and cute, and for making me laugh. *This has to work. Stop fighting against this,* I tried telling myself. *I really like you,* I whispered into his mouth as we kissed hoping saying the words out loud might make them true. I had heard this on an episode of a show adjacent to *The O.C.* and I thought this was what girls were supposed to say. He pulled my shirt gently over my head and put his hand on my skin. My eyes couldn't hold his and I concentrated on the tree shadows lining my house and the brightness of the moon. I felt lightheaded for all the wrong reasons and I wanted to run away from my body. While I hated myself for not feeling even a twinge of arousal, I forced myself to stay put in the hopes that arousal would wash over me with enough time.

The following weekend Alissa drove down for a visit and my body completely eased when I saw her dumpy car chugging up my street. I let a breath out, that I didn't know I had been holding in, and my shoulders dropped two inches from a release of tension. The entire weekend felt like a date I actually wanted to participate in. Every moment felt natural and giddy. We held our eye contact too long for friends and every time she touched my arm or sat her leg against mine my whole body lit up. I had enough energy from her presence to power a small town. Over two bowls of shared pasta, we talked about Ryan and she encouraged me to keep seeing him. My heart sank but I nodded and mumbled something about how all my friends like him and maybe she can meet him next time. That night I nestled my head into her back as we fell asleep in my full size bed. *Why she doesn't sleep at the end of the hall in our guestroom?* my mom innocently asked. *Seems awfully small for two grown girls.*

*I need to take control coz my mind is on a roll And it isn't listening to me. Save me.*

Though he didn't make my body light up or my muscles relax, I trudged forward with my mission to normalcy and saw Ryan quasi–regularly for the next month. He was smart, sweet, and appeared genuinely interested in me. He always paid for dinners and routinely asked, *is this okay?* before doing more physically. His skin felt too hard to me; his hands too rough and I hated the way his 5 o'clock shadow felt on my face and neck, but I didn't stop seeing him. I had convinced myself that one more kiss, laugh, or interesting conversation would hook me and I'd feel that tinge of something, anything that would help my mind stay away from the thought of her. I stayed in my head the whole time we hooked up, keeping a mental tally of what felt good and what felt like nothing. It was mostly nothing.

I spent time considering what seemed to be my only options for a future romantic life, being alone or being with a nice man who I don't care about. Whether it's Ryan or some other Ryan in the future, I began realizing I wouldn't be able to force feelings on some guy. This realization was overwhelming. While my family was liberal and already supportive of my gay uncle, I couldn't fathom the idea of actually being a lesbian. My friends and people I knew at school used words like *dyke* and *fag*, which made me cringe, and I couldn't bear the idea of everyone thinking I was gross. My chest felt like it had been turned into a fist. I drank excessively that summer and it made everything a little easier. There were moments when the drinking was so effective that I thought I was having a great time with Ryan and had feelings for him. These feelings always dissipated when I woke up and once again didn't care if he called or not. He eventually figured me out and knew that I didn't care about seeing him. It appeared to him like I only cared about having a sober driver and someone to make out with at the end of the night, which wasn't completely untrue. It became harder to feign interest on my part so we mutually stop seeing each other. The summer was coming to an end and I hadn't felt the slightest ping of desire for anyone other than her. I didn't know how I would go back to school with this blaring realization. It felt like for the first time I couldn't hide from myself. I tried not calling her as much but then I just thought about her more. I tried to give in and just allow my thoughts to flow, but this would make me become overly excited about a fictitious future.

> *Why would I think such things, Crazy thoughts have quick wings, Gaining momentum fast, One minute I am fine, The next I've lost my mind, To a fake fantasy.*

Occasionally, I allowed myself to live in my head, just to peek into what our life could look like as a couple. In this fantasy we live open, out, and happy. We hold hands and make out drunkenly in front of everyone at house parties. We act like the couples we always make fun of and no one calls me a *dyke* and my friends don't leave me. I wake up sweating from a nightmare in which I've told her I love her and she responds with disgust and she then refuses to speak to me anymore. In my alternate nightmare I try to kiss her and she screams. I have to hide this disgusting truth.

By the last few weeks of summer, my friends began to notice the way I don't actively seek out guys when we're out at bars. I keep to my drink and myself and make excuse after excuse. I stopped dancing altogether at clubs, as I could no longer feign enjoying some guy putting his hands all over me and pretending to be interested in the typical interaction. They continued wondering out loud what was going on with me, but allowed me to make vague remarks like *I'm working on myself* or *I am texting a boy from school.*

School started in two weeks and I hadn't managed to achieve any of my summer goals. Plan A had completely fallen through and I was exhausted. There wasn't enough alcohol to make me stop worrying and I wondered how I would cope being back on campus with her. An inability to hide from myself overwhelmed me and I knew things would never be the same.

I couldn't pretend any longer.

# Firsts

*We all have feelings for our girlfriends, Dana, it doesn't mean you have to act on them.*

—Sharon Fairbanks, <u>The L Word</u>, 2004

I first met my wife at our weekly sorority pledge class meetings. She hardly spoke a word, but managed to befriend one of the louder, more opinionated girls in our cohort. The two of them showed up everywhere together and I immediately decided I didn't like her based on her friend selection. Alissa was one of the few girls who consistently aced our weekly tests and always volunteered for upcoming events. I assumed she was a straight–laced nerd. During a meeting, I rolled my eyes at her as she perfectly rattled off the Greek Alphabet a week before the auditory test was due.

I first spoke to my wife at our annual sorority Halloween party. Five of us pledges had dressed up as Mad Dog wine coolers (an homage to the sisters who actively hazed us with these noxious drinks). We primped and pregrammed at Jamie's*, the opinionated–loudmouth, apartment. I needed help pinning my dress and Alissa was the only girl around not applying mountains of makeup or re–curling her hair. The bathroom sizzled with bad lights, blow dryers, and girls chattering, so the two of us stepped into a bedroom to cool down and complete my outfit.

It was the first time we had ever been alone and I didn't intend on liking her; she routinely made all of us look stupid and lazy at our weekly meetings and her quietness felt off putting. However, it quickly became obvious that hating her would be tough. With just two of us, she spoke – and was surprisingly hilarious. Her humor came out and it was biting, her neuroticism appeared, and she was silly in a way most adults could no longer access. A sudden charge moved from the bottom of my toes to the top of my head as she carefully safety–pinned my dress and chatted away. I felt flustered as she kept her hand on my thigh fidgeting the safety pin into just the correct place. Turned out she was also a bit of a perfectionist. I held my breath and felt my heartbeat quicken from the weight of her hand on me as I tried my best to remain fixed in place. It happened that once we started talking we realized we had a few things in common, and more interestingly I just liked how I felt around her. There was something about her that I was drawn to and wanted to be around. For the rest of the night we were inseparable. Although I'm sure I did, I don't recall speaking to anyone else at the party that night. I only remember standing around a keg, staring at her, and memorizing every word that left her mouth. After the party sizzled out, we were forced to separate due to obligations with various friends.

*Don't leave* I said, in all seriousness as we headed down opposite streets. She was headed out for late night snacks with her gregarious sidekick, while Meredith and I made our way to another party.

*I wish I didn't have to* she said with complete sincerity.

I'm pretty sure I watched her walk away hoping she would turn around and change her mind. When I came home that night, I wrote on her Facebook wall: *I am completely obsessed with youuuu!!!!* For the next hour, I attentively scrolled through every photo on her Facebook account, twice; digging for personal details. I knew she didn't have a boyfriend at the moment, but wanted to see if anyone looked important from her past. Her pictures primarily displayed photos of her and her friends. In her pictures she appeared at ease and preppy. Without a boy in a single frame, a startling sense relief settled in.

The year we met, she regularly styled her hair half up with a front bump and doused herself in Juicy perfume. I was smitten. The first time I understood the immensity of my wife's magnetic pull occurred the morning after the Halloween party. Immediately we began spending all of our time together. We let most of our other obligations and friendships fall to the wayside. My best friend, understandably, began to hate me for ditching her practically overnight, but I couldn't help it! Being around Alissa was the most addictive thing that I had ever experienced and I couldn't manage staying away from her more than a few hours. Over the next few months we talked nonstop and with the eagerness of investigative reporters. We were equally engrossed in learning everything about one another in meticulous detail. There wasn't enough information about her to fill me up. I loved watching her interact with the world around us as her actions deviated from most people I surrounded myself with, especially myself.

She has the moral compass of a nun and an outrageous amount of self–respect — foreign concepts to me. I once saw her find a $10 bill and automatically hand it to a homeless townie before it could even reach her pocket. *We could have bought two forties and a pizza slice with that!* I said whining. When we first met she had never skipped class, though eventually I would persuade her to take part in this small act of rebellion. I found out I might as well have let her go to class as she stressed out and hung to guilt for the entire hour she missed. Alissa wouldn't even sneak cookies out of the dining hall. *It's stealing,* she would say as I laughed and took two.

On a typical, drunk Thursday night, a group of us sat in a frat house, passing around a Frisbee full of cocaine. Making a disgusted face, Alissa handed the Frisbee to the next sister. Peer pressure left her unmoved while I prayed for it; I craved any excuse for more: more drugs, more drinks, more meaningless sex. While we didn't immediately understand one another's behavior we had a deep fascination in our asymmetry. We carried opposing types of emotional baggage. Her splintered nuclear family caused her to shut off any thought of romantic entanglements, while my childhood trauma left me seeking out empty sex and various other forms of self–harm. We presented ourselves to the world as opposites. While I acted brash and open for anything, she presented as reserved and only participated in activities that felt right for her. Alissa instinctively had a well–developed ability to listen to her mind and body that I found incredibly attractive.

With time, we discovered that while we masked ourselves differently to the world, our internal truths mirrored one another precisely. As young women we were both a bit broken, angry, and mistrustful of people around us. Slowly, we started to patch up our own emotional cracks with each other's help. Being around her began to make me feel whole.

———————————

The first time I tried to kiss my wife, she shot me down. It was late and we lounged in my bed drunk on the edge of sleep, but still awake laughing. Sensations of lust, love, and need washed over me as I thoughtless leaned over to kiss her. *Please don't kiss me,* she said quietly. The words punched me in the throat and reddened me with embarrassment. In the protection of the dark room I played the devastating incident coolly and didn't let her see that I was literally dying of embarrassment. I wanted to jump out my window, crawl under our crawlspace, and never be seen or heard of again. Knowing she couldn't see the heat radiating off my face brought a miniscule amount of comfort and allowed me to rally up a faux disinterest. *You're such a prude,* I said shoving her shoulder with a weird laugh-snort as if we were two bros.

Before the sun reemerged to start its day, Alissa had crept out my bed and gone back to her apartment. It was the weekend, which normally meant the two of us would wake up late together, side by side, hungover but happy. I felt horrified and my inner dialogue was reeling with disgust at myself. How could I have done something so horrifying? I no longer wanted meaningless guys and hookups. I only wanted her and I hated myself for it.

Two years later, our relationship started feeling even more convoluted. Her bed was the only place I wanted to be. It reached an apex where I would have sex with a guy, kick him out, and then arrive at her house 30 minutes later just to fall asleep. This routine was expected. *Where are you?* She would text me if I hadn't made it to her house by 2 a.m. The sex I was having began feeling intolerable. I hated their masculine smells and how rough their skin felt against me. A new habit formed where I showered maniacally seconds after they left and immediately throw my sheets in the wash. I needed to wash the experience off of my things and myself. Their testosterone lingered everywhere, and at times might have been imagined, proved difficult to get rid of. No amount of scrubbing could wash her out of my system. I was going insane.

During the first semester back of my senior year, my drinking and rage reached another new apex. The summer of forcing myself to have feelings for any male had proven unsuccessful. Until this point, I had never failed at anything I had set out to accomplish. I was a sloppy drunk and loathing myself. On nights that she didn't stop me from sleeping with guys, I was furious at her and myself. While I couldn't stomach this self–destructive merry–go–ride any longer I couldn't figure out a way to get off it. Many nights ended with me yelling at her about nothing other than a deep internal need to make noise and chaos. I was nasty and my attempts to make her feel awful worked. I drank because I hated that I wanted her. I drank to try to kill my feelings for her or at least shove them down to a place where I couldn't feel them, but this never worked. I was afraid if I didn't yell I'd break down and tell her everything. The yelling, while unfair, felt refreshing. I was mad about so many things. Suddenly, anything more than kissing with guys started to make me feel physically ill, but I kept at it in the hopes something would change.

Alissa's true feelings for me became harder for her to repress. She became a calculated cockblock; taking my phone when she knew a guy was texting me, and luring me to her apartment with promises of late-night pizza. I feigned annoyance, but secretly savored her obvious intentions. At our third Halloween party together, this time dressed up as characters from Mario Kart, we split a fifth of vodka and flirted shamelessly. A switch had flipped and we finally kissed. The kissing went on for months. It was every cliché I had ever heard come to realization. The frustration of not being able to crawl into her skin was maddening. Close was never enough.

The night before winter break only the two of us occupied the sorority house. Everyone had left for vacation while we generated bogus excuses to our families to stay on campus for one more night.

I remember eating clementines in her kitchen at 3 a.m.; starved from all the kissing. The sweet floral scents lingered.

My feet felt cold against the vinyl floor and a draft

pushed through the backdoor. Alissa and I stood staring and laughing at one another feeling high off the pheromones. I had never kissed someone I had real feelings for and suddenly the whole world seemed brighter and louder than I remembered.

No one had cleaned a dish in months and the sink pilled up with 100 meals worth of crusty cutlery. The countertops were sticky from spilt liquor. The floors stuck too. The garbage needed to be taken out, and I had never been happier.

# Acknowledgements

To my parents, who have taken my written work seriously since childhood and have always celebrated creative efforts. Thank you for making reading and words an important part of our home. Thanks to my brother Parker for being a life long best friend and source of creative energy. To Alissa, for seeing me and loving me. You are my safest, happiest place.

Thank you to my editor Samantha Atzeni for helping to strengthen my voice and give my work a clear direction. Your encouragement, thoughtful ideas, and openness made this process a true joy. Thank you to everyone at Read Furiously for giving this collection a home.

If you can't love yourself, how the hell you gonna love somebody else?

**–RuPaul**

# Samantha Mann

Samantha writes personal and nonfiction essays covering LGBTQ life, mental health, and feminism. Her work can be found on BUST, Emry's Journal, The Establishment, Bustle, and Washington Post Magazine. Samantha lives with her wife in Brooklyn, NY.

# A Note to our Furious Readers

From all of us at Read Furiously, we hope you enjoyed our latest title, *Putting Out: Essays on Otherness*.

There are countless narratives in this world and we would like to share as many of them as possible with our Furious Readers.

It is with this in mind that we pledge to donate a portion of these book sales to causes that are special to Read Furiously and the creators involved in *Putting Out*. These causes are chosen with the intent to better the lives of others who are struggling to tell their own stories.

Reading is more than a passive activity – it is the opportunity to play an active role within our world. At Read Furiously, its editors and its creators wish to add an active voice to the world we all share because we believe any growth within the company is aimless if we can't also nurture positive change in our local and global communities. The causes we support are not politically driven, but are culturally and socially–based to encourage a sense of civic responsibility associated with the act of reading. Each cause has been researched thoroughly, discussed openly, and voted upon carefully by our team of Read Furiously editors.

The author has asked Read Furiously to donate the proceeds from this work to benefit the Women's Resource Center in Radford, Virginia.

The Women's Resource Center in Radford Virginia is a community–based center providing a variety of vital no cost services to women and children. As a college student I was able to receive counseling services that I wouldn't have been able to afford otherwise in a safe and nurturing environment. Helping women heal from trauma and violence is the first steps in women accessing their voice. We cannot share our narratives and connect with one another until our voices have been reclaimed. The Women's Resource Center is a vital part of the Radford community lifting up with thousands of women and families each year.

To find out more about who, what, why, and where Read Furiously lends its support, please visit our website at readfuriously.com/charity

Happy reading and giving, Furious Readers!

## Read Often, Read Well, Read Furiously!

CPSIA information can be obtained
at www.ICGtesting.com
Printed in the USA
BVHW041755180219
540556BV00018B/258/P